Orangeville Ontario Book 3 in Colour Photos, Saving Our History One Photo at a Time

Photography
by Barbara Raué
2013

Series Name:
Cruising Ontario

Book 52: Orangeville Book 3

Cover photo: Eagle Carving in front of 299 Broadway Avenue

Series Name: Cruising Ontario
Saving Our History One Photo at a Time

Photos now in full colour
Check the Appendixes in the back of each book for
descriptions of architectural terms and building styles

Book 33: Southampton
Book 34: Jarvis
Book 35: Hagersville
Book 37: Simcoe
Book 38: Cambridge Part 1 – Galt Book 1
Book 39: Cambridge Part 1 – Galt Book 2
Book 40: Cambridge Part 2 – Preston
Book 41: Cambridge Part 3 – Hespeler
Book 42: Kitchener Book 1
Book 43: Kitchener Book 2
Book 46: Shelburne
Book 47: Alton, Mono and Caledon
Book 48: London in Colour
Book 50: Orangeville Beginnings in Colour
Book 51: Orangeville on Broadway in Colour
Book 52: Orangeville Book 3 in Colour
Book 53: Dundas in Colour Book 1
Book 54: Dundas in Colour Book 2
Book 55: Dundas in Colour Book 3
Book 56: Stratford
Book 57: Hanover

Other Books by Barbara Raue

Coins of Gold

Arrows, Indians and Love

The Life and Times of Barbara
Volume 1: Inventions That Have Enhanced My Life
Volume 2: Entertainment That I Have Enjoyed
Volume 3: East Coast Trips
Volume 4: Olympics Have Always Intrigued Me
Volume 5: Wonders of the World
Volume 6: Caribbean Cruises We Have Enjoyed
Volume 7: Animals
Volume 8: Storms and Other Major Disasters in My Lifetime
Volume 9: Wars, Terrorist Attacks and Major Disasters

The Cromwell Family Book

Orangeville

In 1837 James Griggs bought 100 acres on the south side of what is now Broadway and built the first mill on Mill Creek. In 1843, Orange Lawrence bought 300 acres along with Griggs' mill; he opened a general store, built a second mill, started the first school, and in 1847 he was the first postmaster. In 1857 two sons-in-law of Orange Lawrence, Thomas Jull and John Walker Reid built a mill at the corner of Mill and Armstrong Streets. In 1863 Orangeville was incorporated as a village in Wellington County with a population of 1200. By 1871 two daily stage lines were operating between Orangeville and Brampton and in the same year the Toronto, Grey and Bruce Railway, a narrow gauge rail line, reached Orangeville. In 1885 telephones were installed in Orangeville, but it wasn't until 1916 that electricity came to the town.

Caledon Village

Caledon is located northwest of Brampton. Caledon Village is one of the small communities in the town of Caledon.

Mono Centre

Mono is a rural community of rolling, tree-covered hills with streams and creeks forming the headwaters of the Humber, Nottawasaga and Credit Rivers. Mono Centre Post Office was open from 1851 to 1969. The Turnbull and Henry families settled here in 1823. The village included a general store, library, hotel, blacksmith, grist mill, saw mill, wagon maker, church, and township hall.

Table of Contents

Zina Street

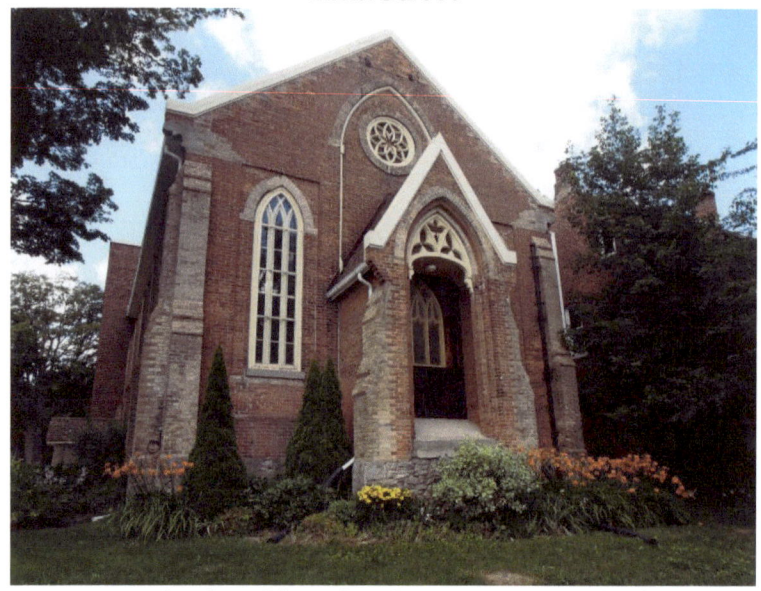

Primitive Methodist Church – 3 Zina Street – built in 1867, a simple Gothic structure with buff brick buttresses separating the segmented lancet windows

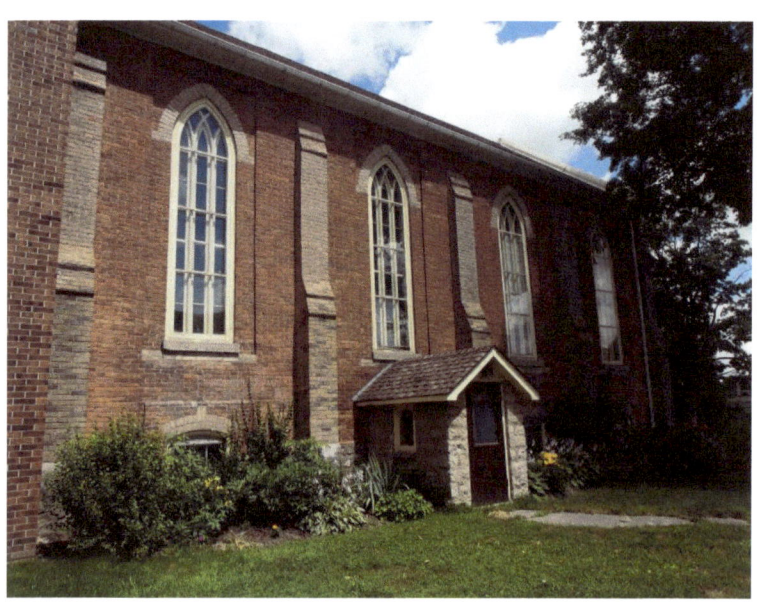

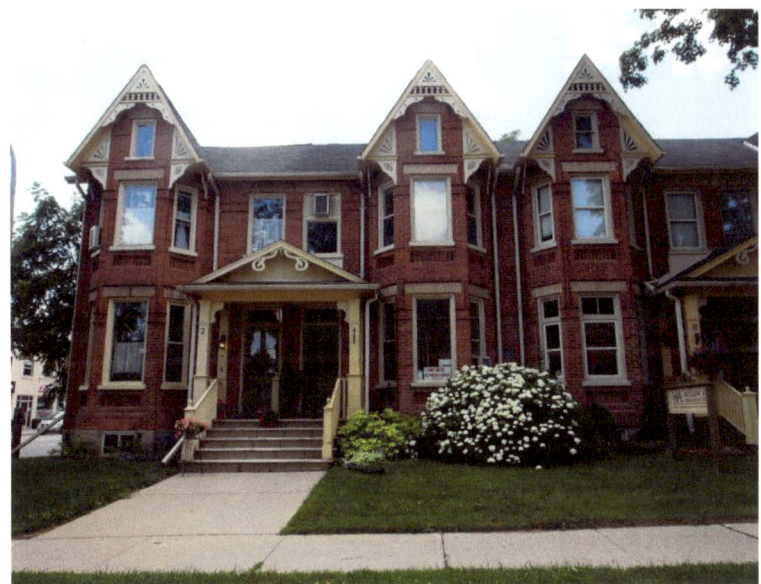

2-6 Zina Street – Queen Anne style with decorative brick panels under the windows and buff brick soldiering topping the windows. Each unit of the row houses has a two-and-a-half storey tower-like bay with projecting eaves and large fretwork pieces resembling brackets. The transom over the off centre doors helps to lighten the interior hallways.

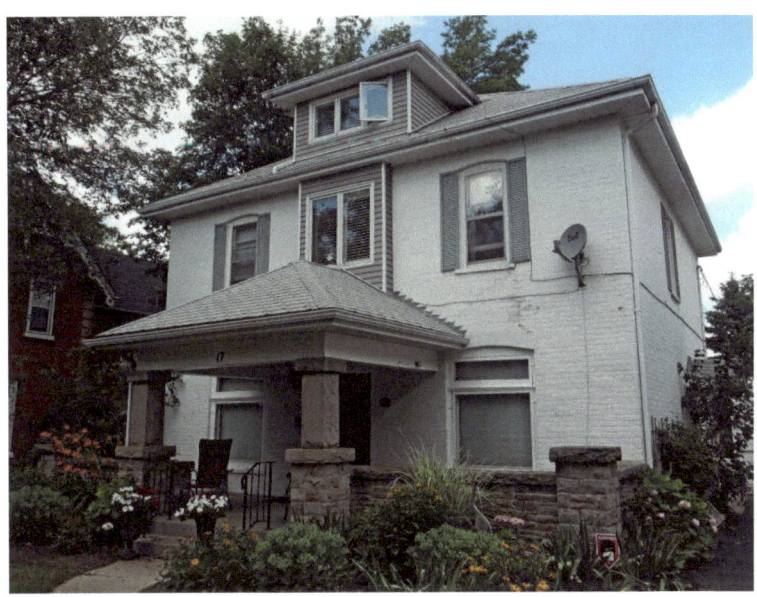

17 Zina Street – Italianate, dormer in attic

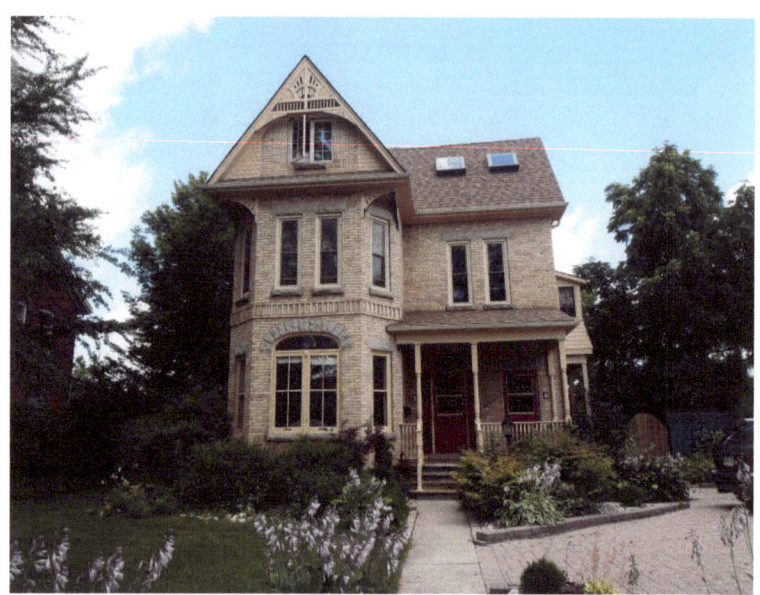

7 Zina Street – built in 1890 using all buff-coloured brick, the home of Jeremiah Dodds, a pharmacist. The style is an interpretation of Victorian Gothic with highly decorated vergeboards and Queen Anne influences in the rectangular windows and heavy stone lintels.

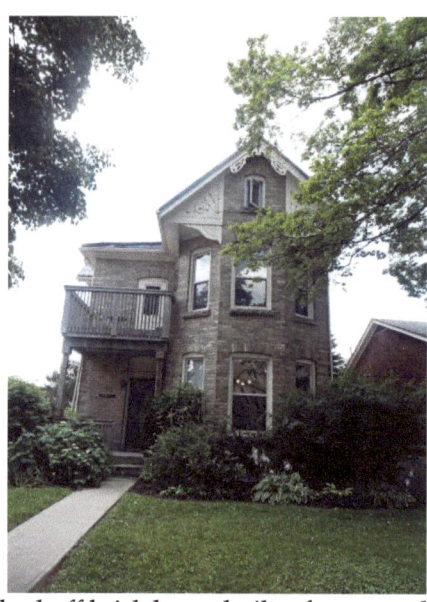

14 Zina – a similar buff brick home built a few years later than 7 Zina, built for merchant John Thompson

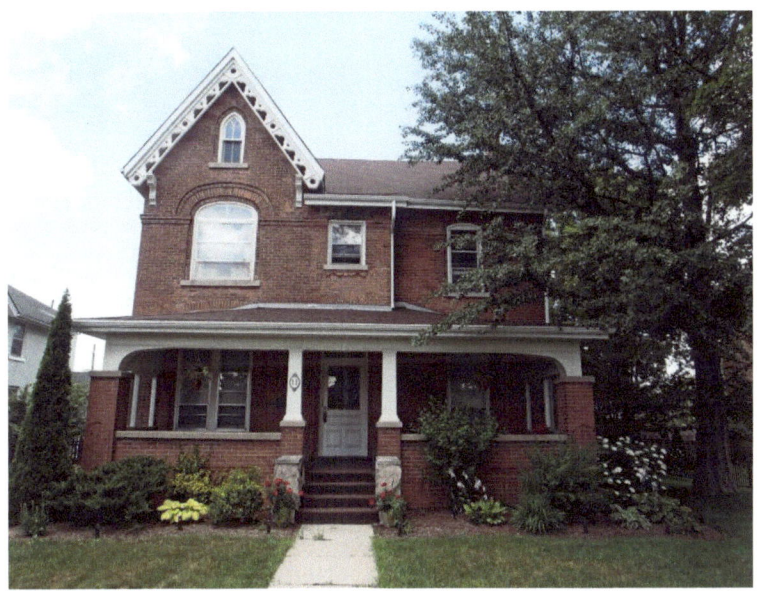

11 Zina – Gothic Revival style with an L-shaped floor plan, front gable and simple lancet window – the wide arch-topped windows topped with transoms came into fashion later in the century. The porch has 1920s features indicating the home has been modified over the years.

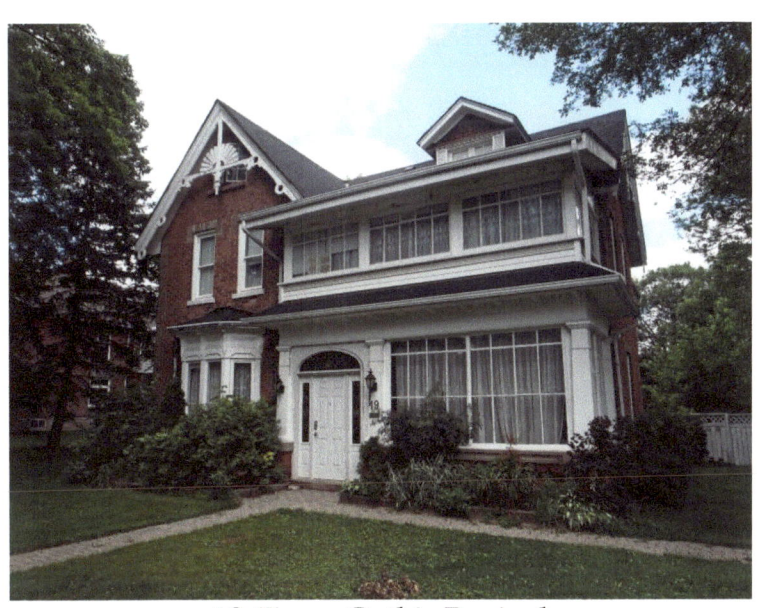

19 Zina – Gothic Revival

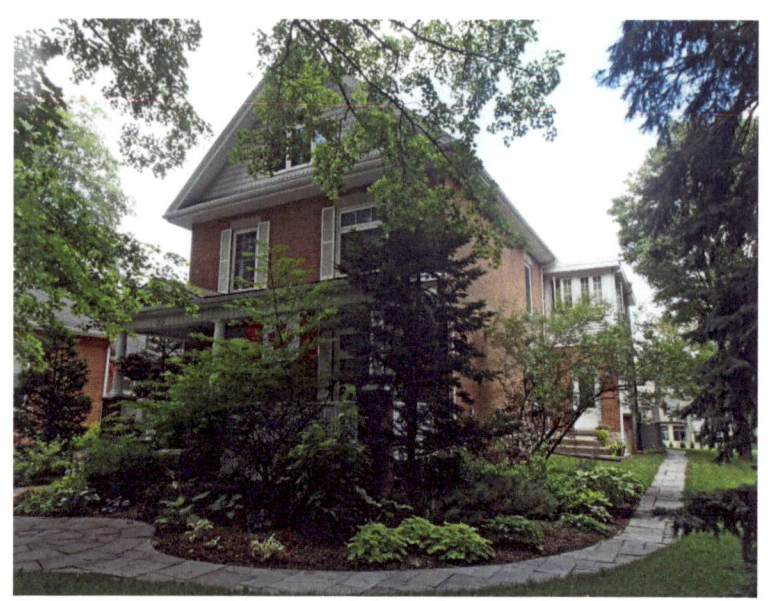

23 Zina – Edwardian style

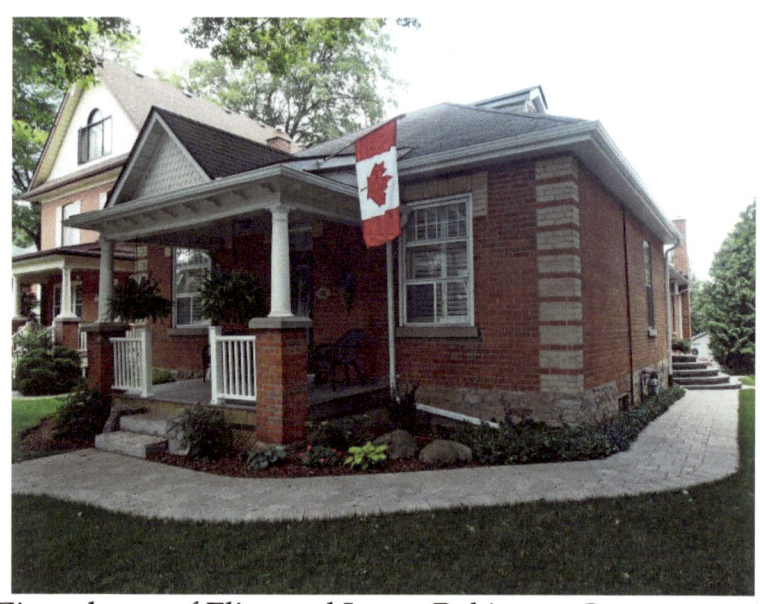

25 Zina – home of Eliza and James Robinson, Carpenter – 1885

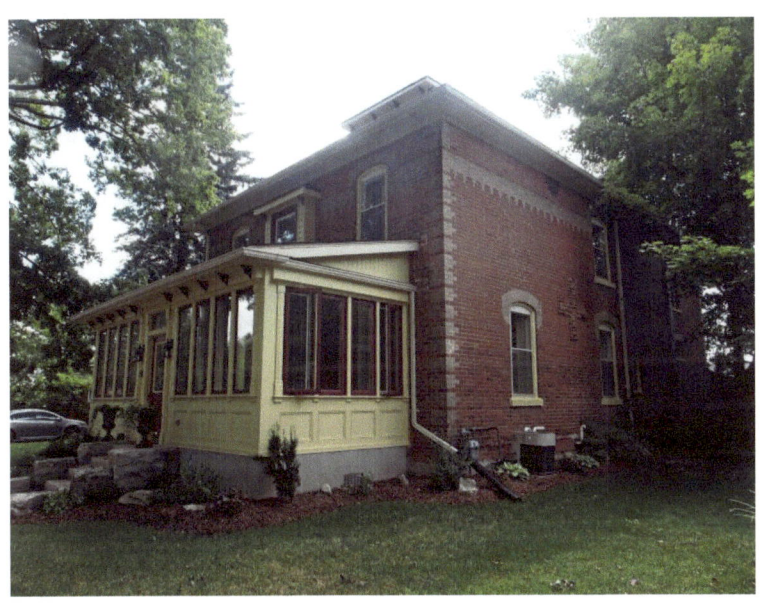

28 Zina - Italianate home built in 1881 by James McDonald with the belvedere topping the hipped roof to bring light into the attic – a rare feature in Orangeville

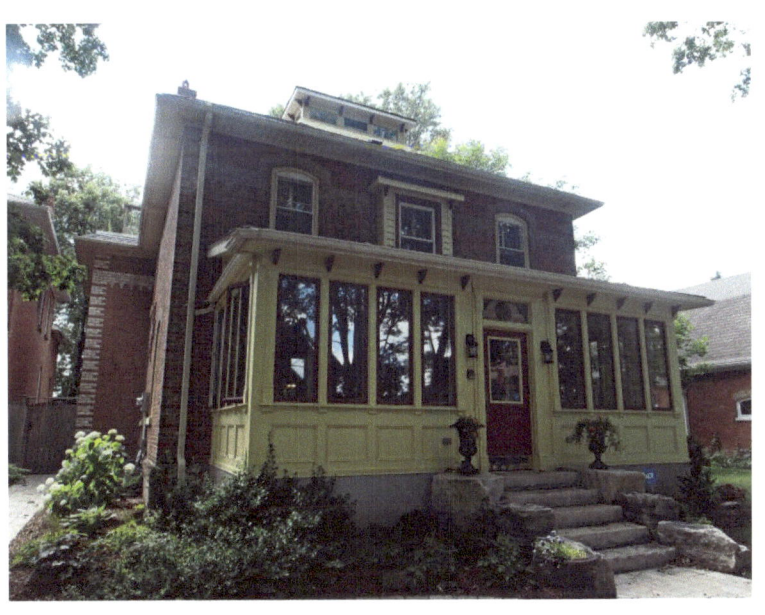

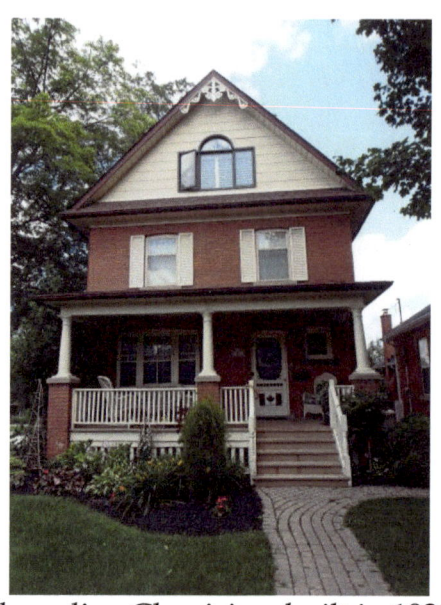

27 Zina – Edwardian Classicism built in 1923 with large triangular front gable with Palladian window and shallow roofed porch

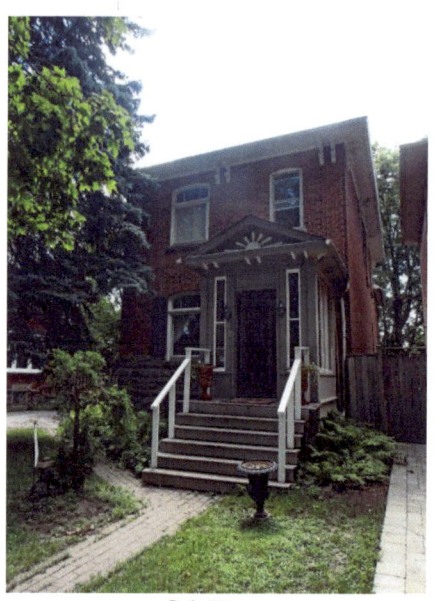

26 Zina

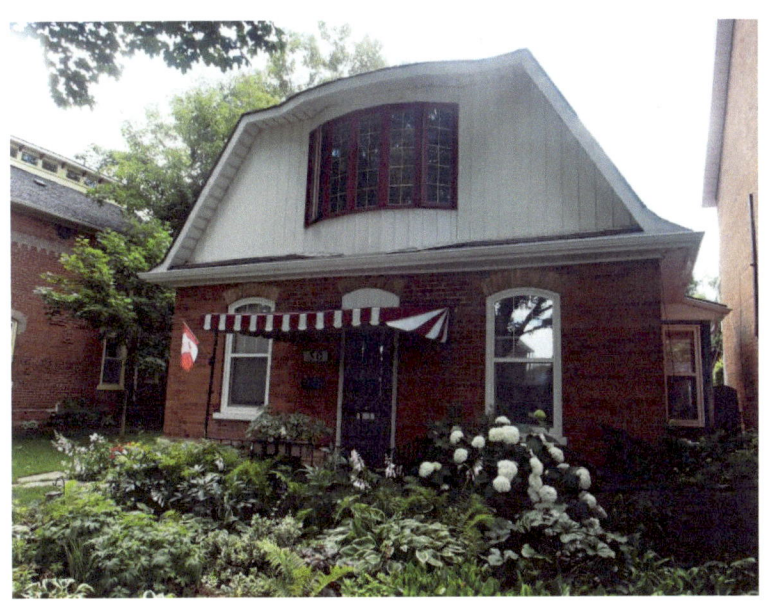

A uniquely shaped roof line – 30 Zina

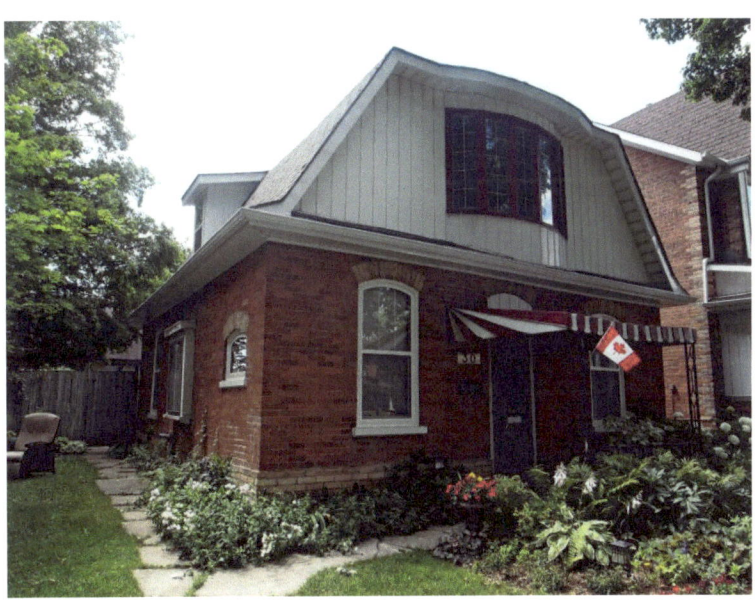

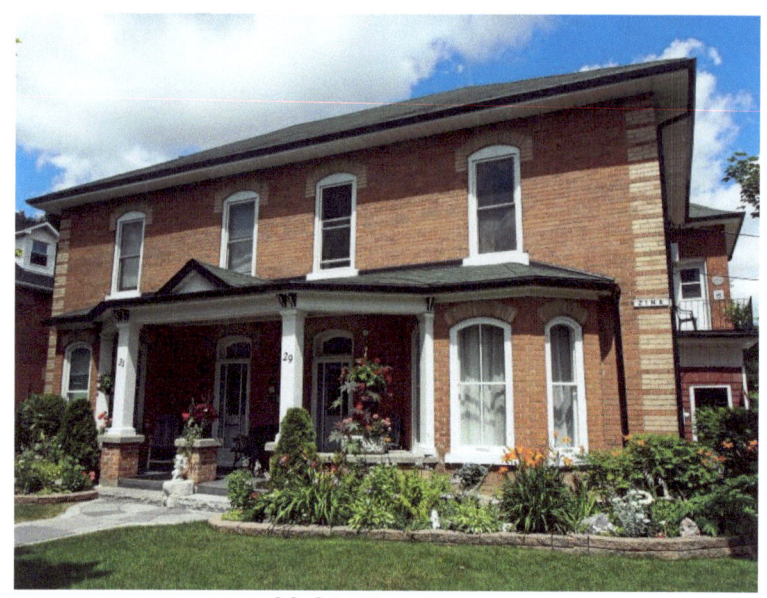

29-31 Zina Street

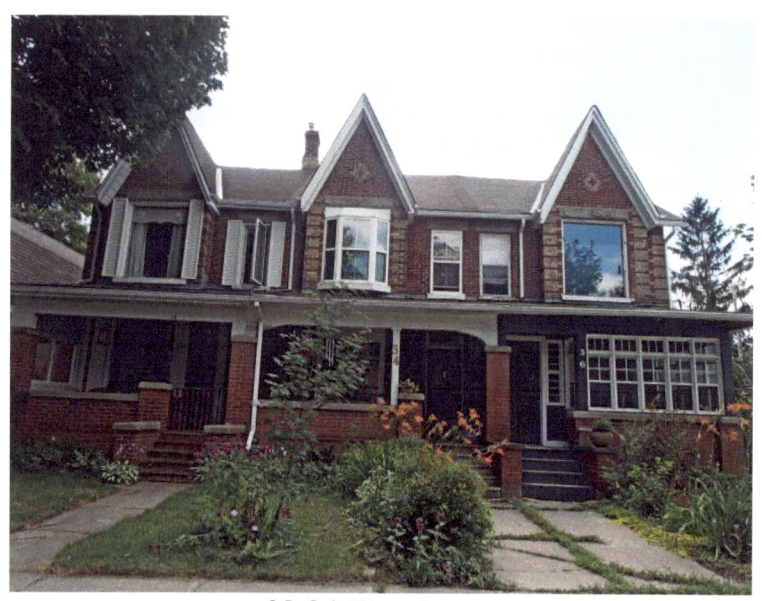

32-36 Zina Street

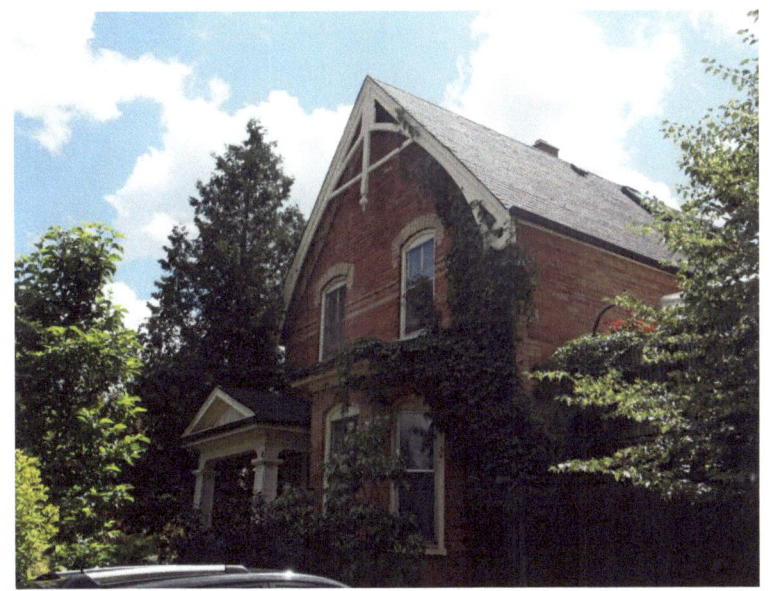

#31 Zina Street – Gothic Revival

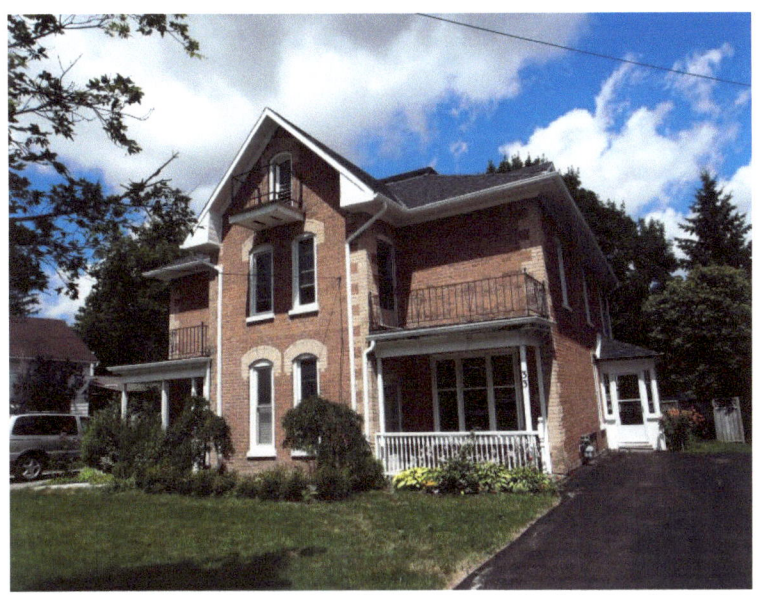

33 Zina – Gothic Revival – dichromatic brickwork, lighter coloured voussoirs

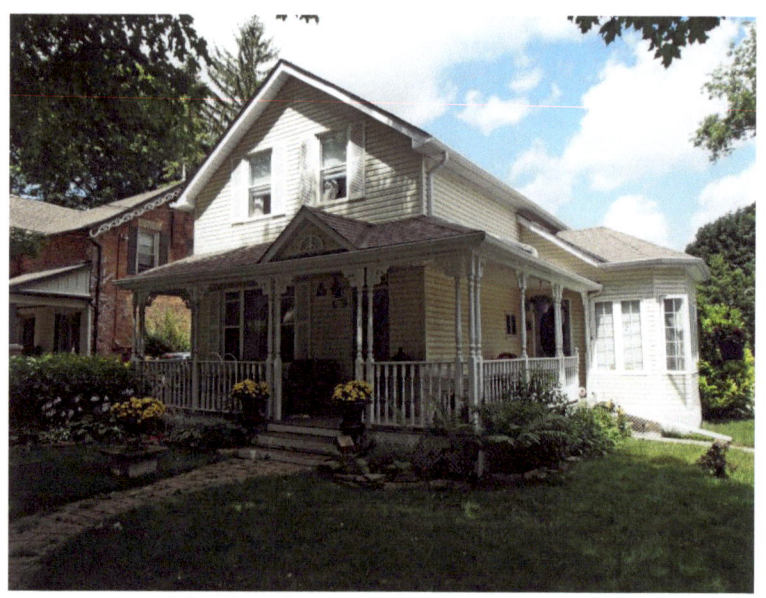

39 Zina Street – Gothic Revival

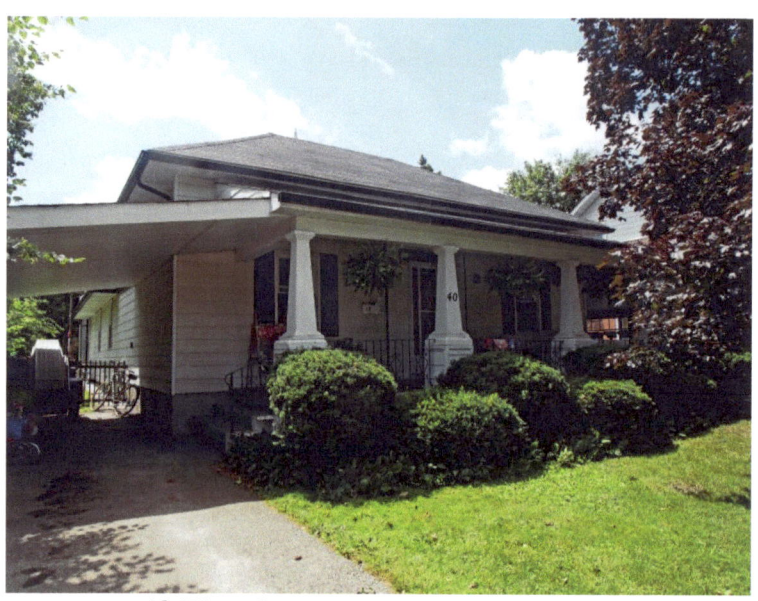

40 Zina Street – one-storey cottage

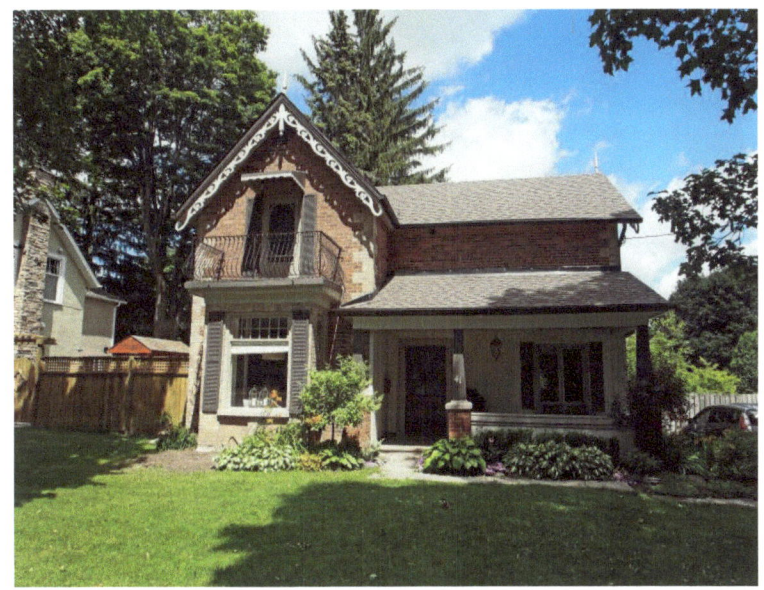

41 Zina – Gothic Revival – larger windows added on first floor
Built in 1877

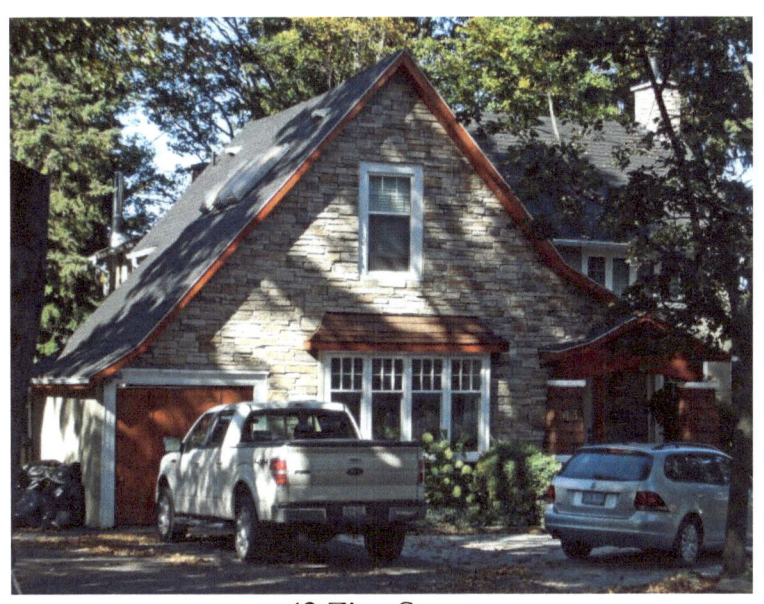

43 Zina Street

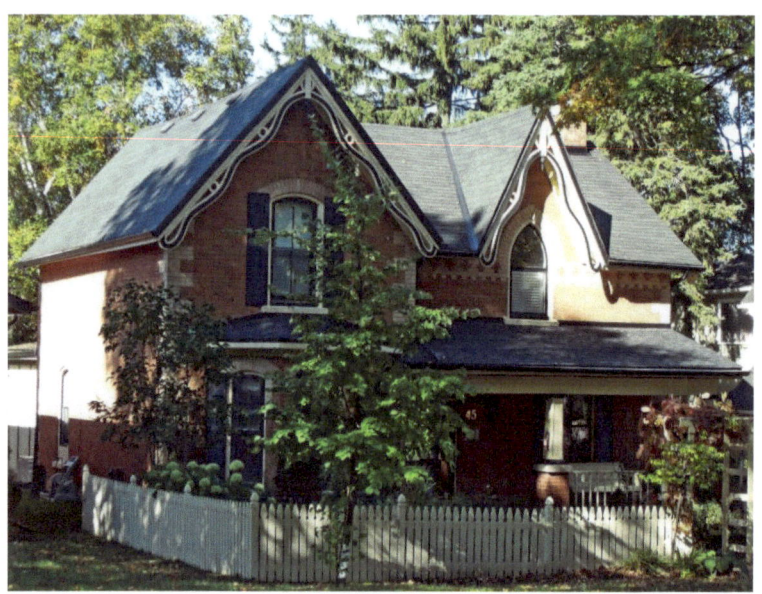

45 Zina Street – Gothic Revival- picture taken in 2011

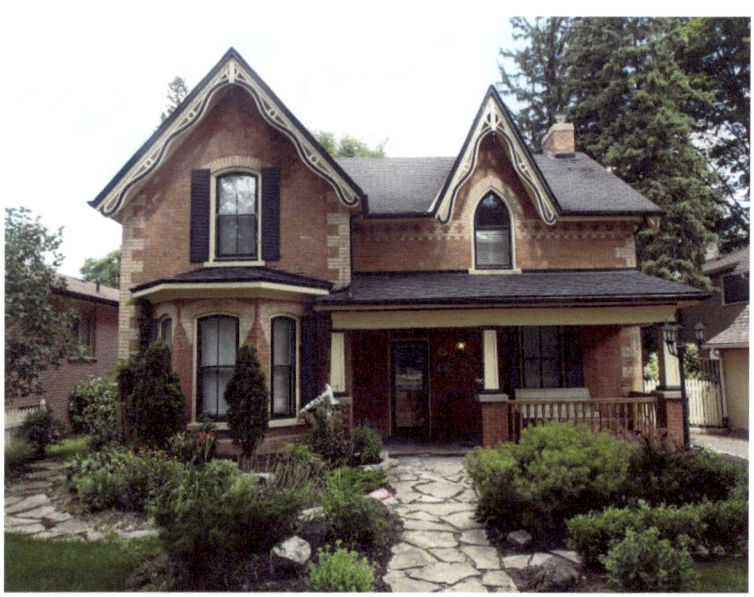

The same house taken in 2013 with new landscaping – what a transformation. Buff brick banding, decorative bargeboard, simple lancet window in the additional front gable. The porch has been altered probably after 1920 – the short brick piers with squared columns reflect Edwardian Classicism common at that time.

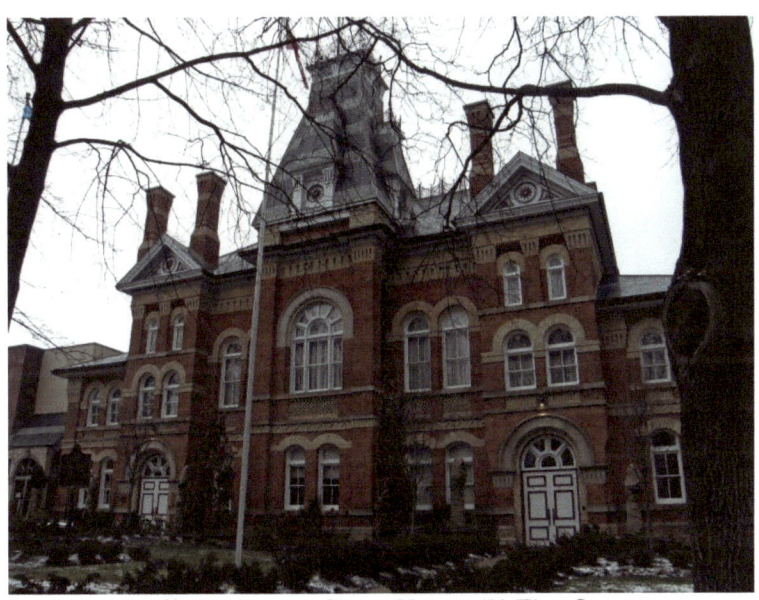

Dufferin County Court House, 51 Zina Street
Classic Revival style built in 1880 with three towers that project from the
façade, the centre one most prominent; buff brick for decorative window
hoods, bands, panels; cornice and capitals on red brick pilasters; projecting
gable ends with triangular pediments and decorated tympanums

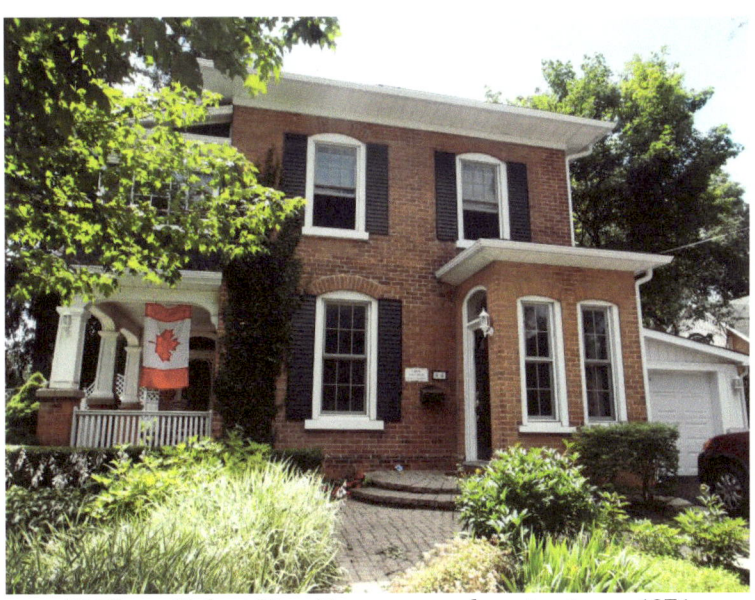

56 Zina – Robert Hewitt, mason and contractor, c. 1876
Italianate style

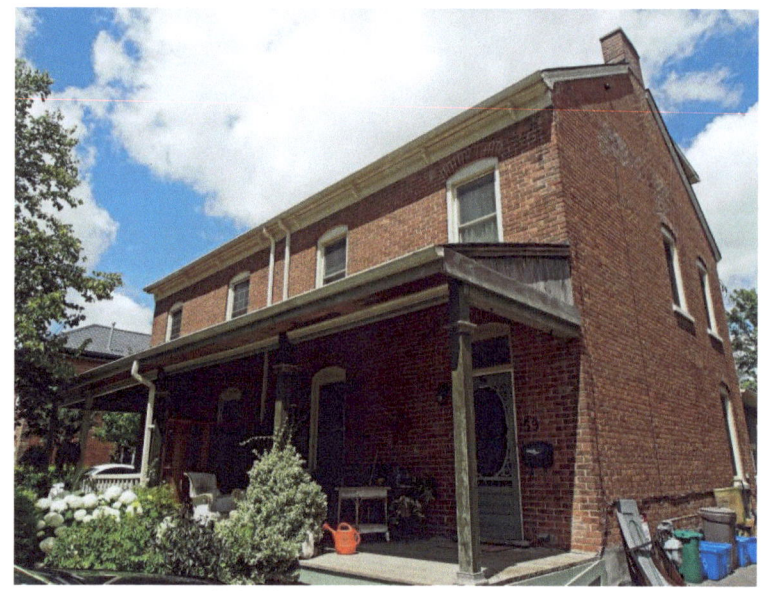

57-59 Zina Street - Gothic

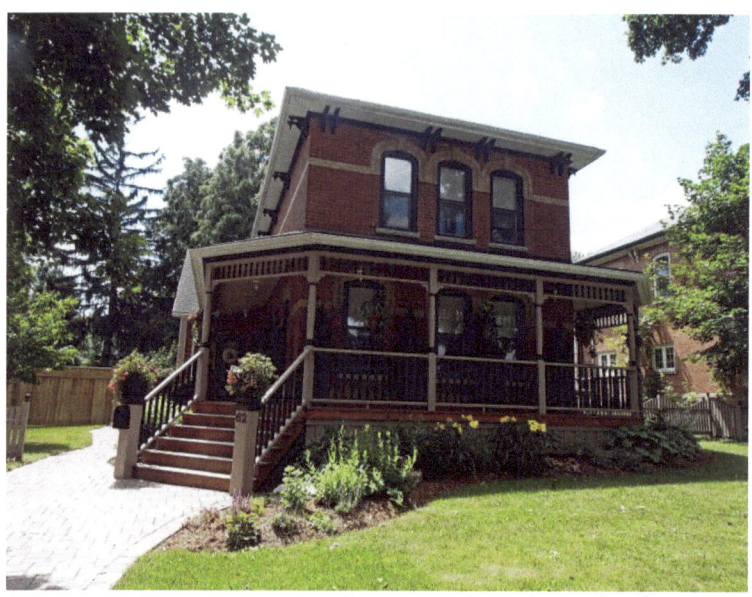

62 Zina – Italianate – paired cornice brackets, buff coloured voussoirs and banding

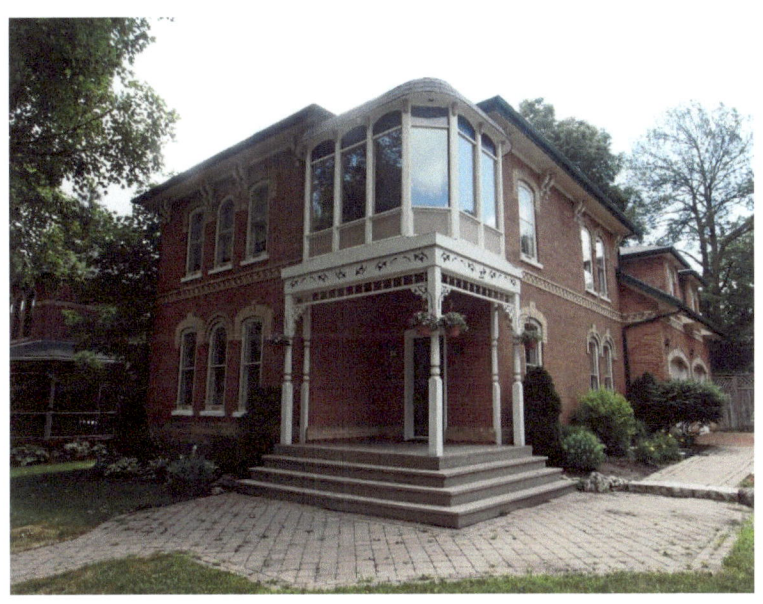

64 Zina Street – Italianate – paired cornice brackets, buff coloured voussoirs and dentil moulding

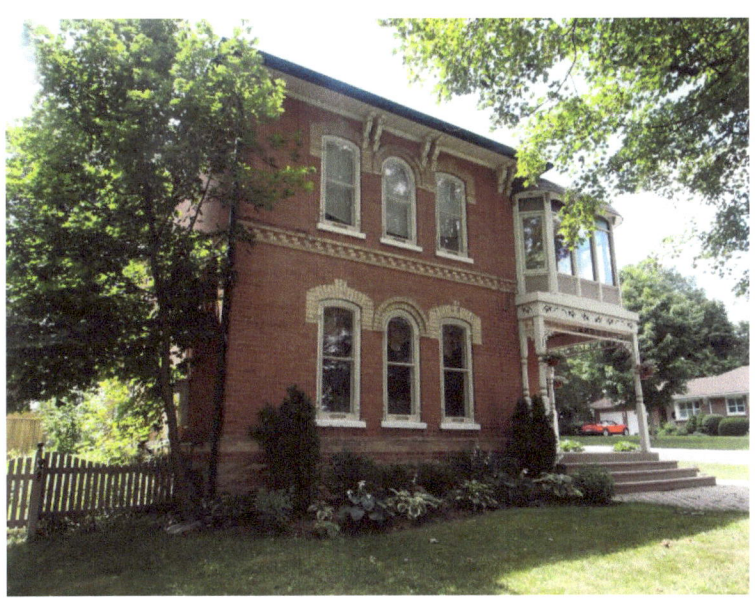

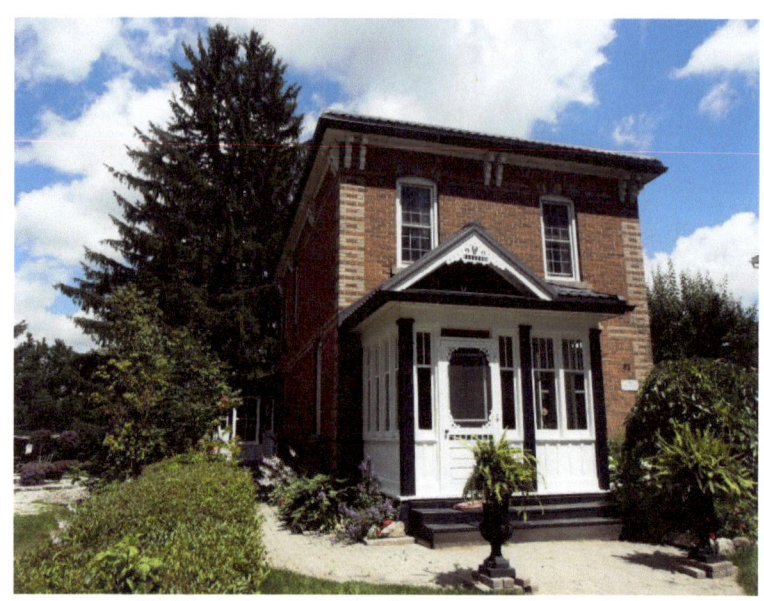

63 Zina Street – Italianate style - 1880
Agnes and Reverend John M. McIntyre, Presbyterian Minister

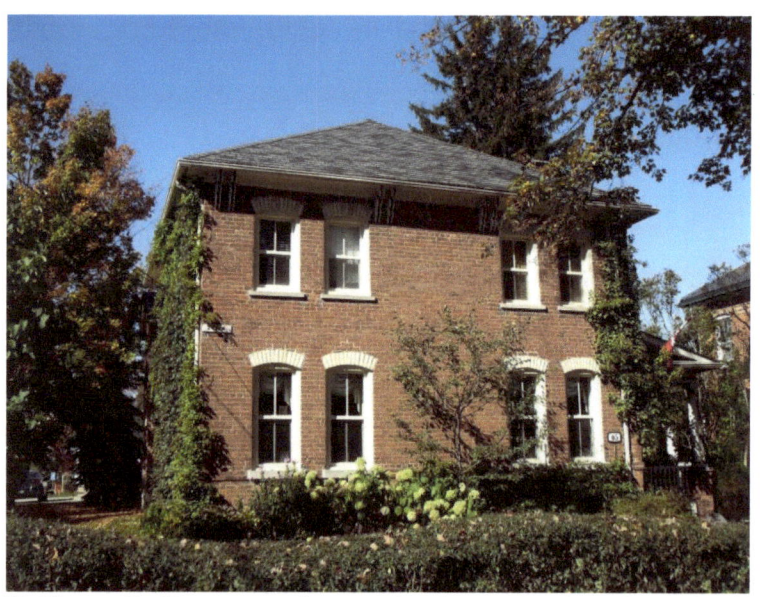

65 Zina – Italianate style – paired cornice brackets, buff-coloured voussoirs

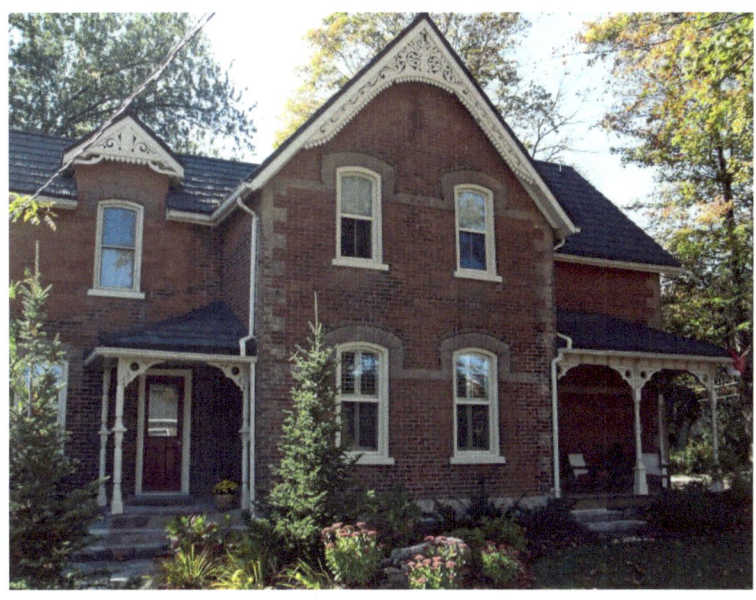

67 Zina – Gothic Revival style with sharply-pitched gables, detailed vergeboards, dichromatic brickwork, corner quoins

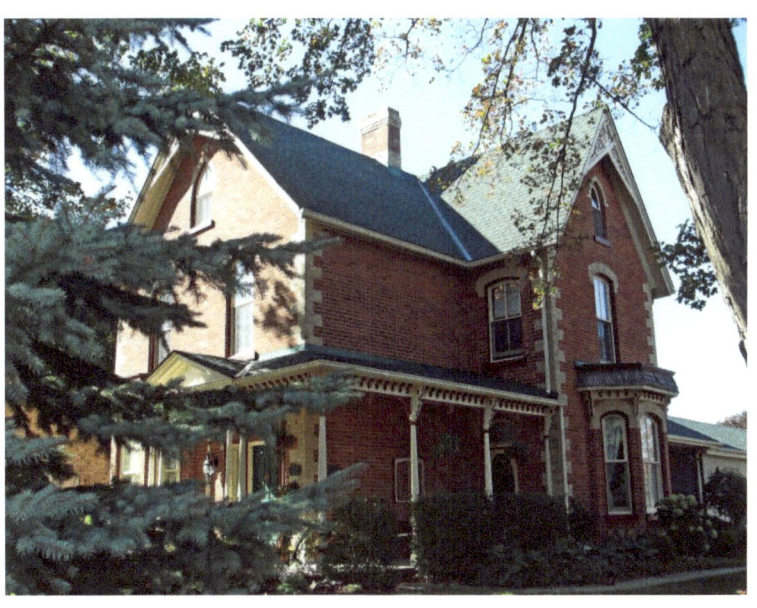

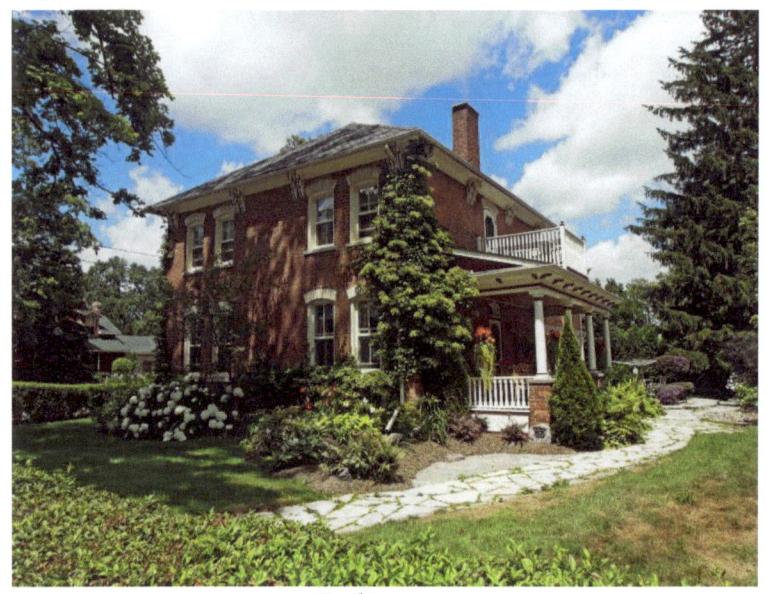

Italianate

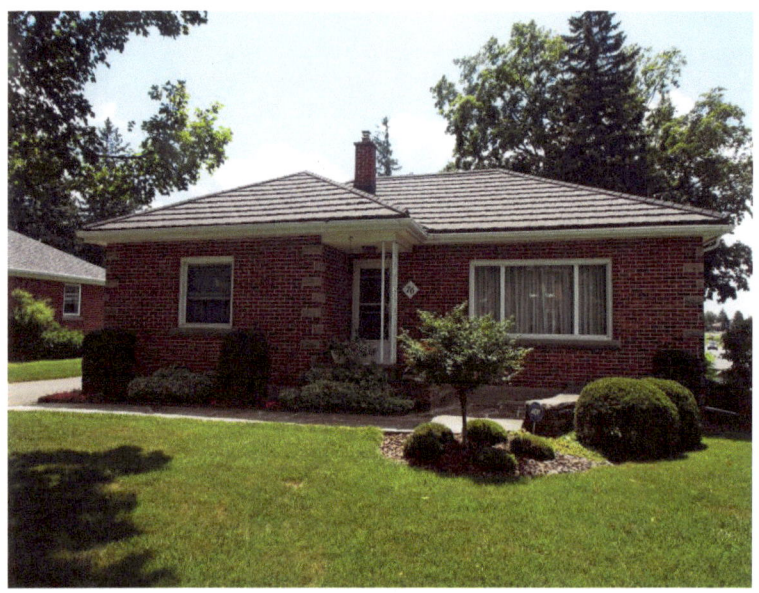

76 Zina Street – cottage

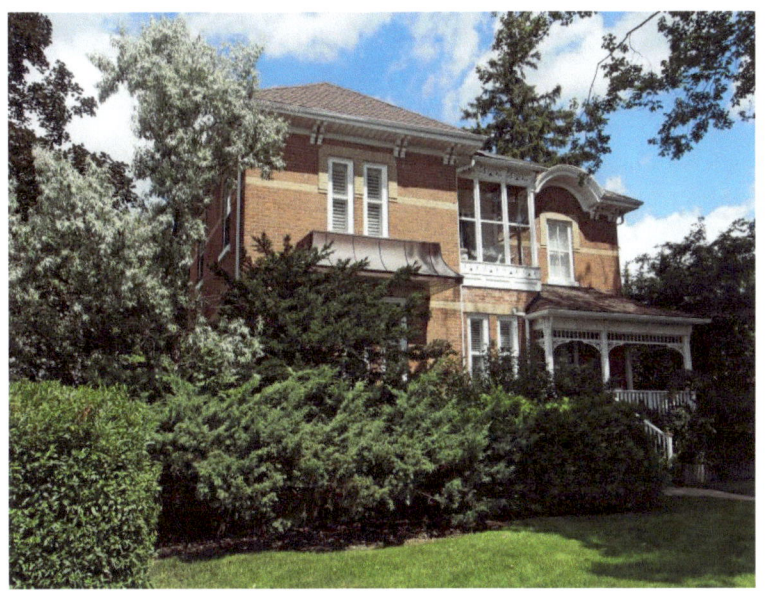

Italianate style

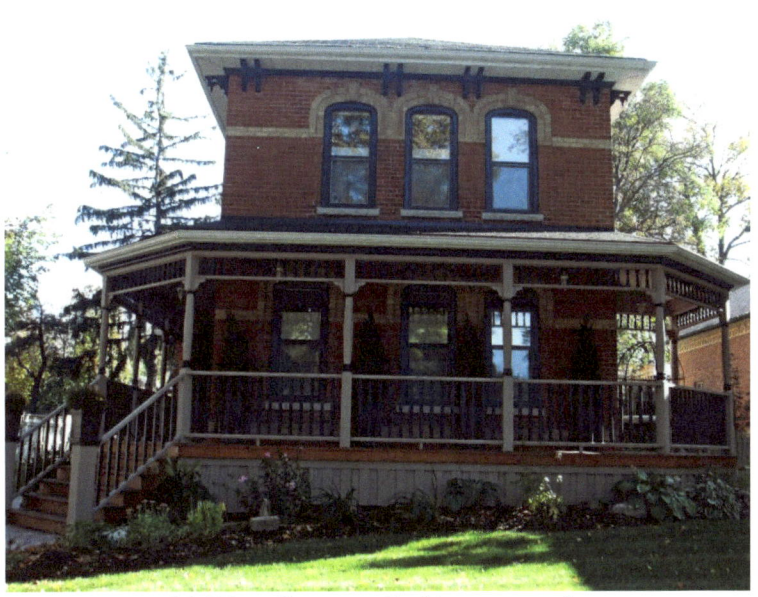

81 Zina Street – Italianate style

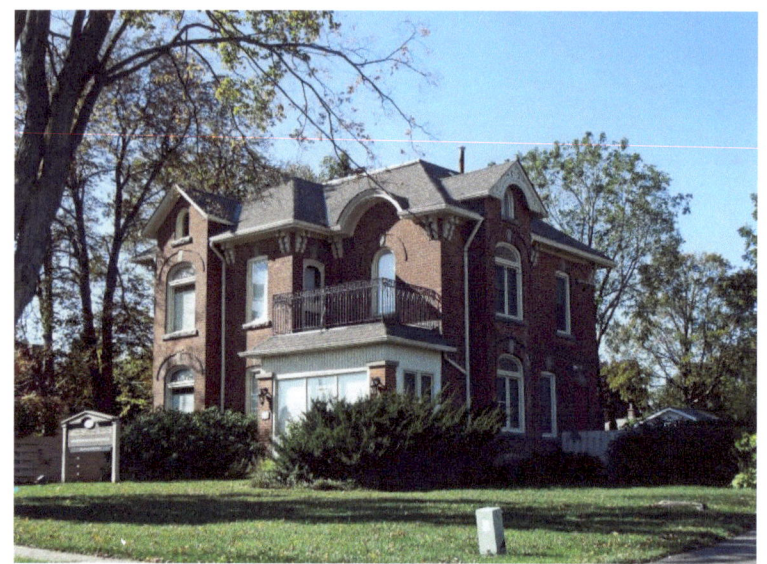

Victorian Gothic with decorated vergeboards and Queen Anne influences in rectangular windows and heavy stone lintels

Clara Street

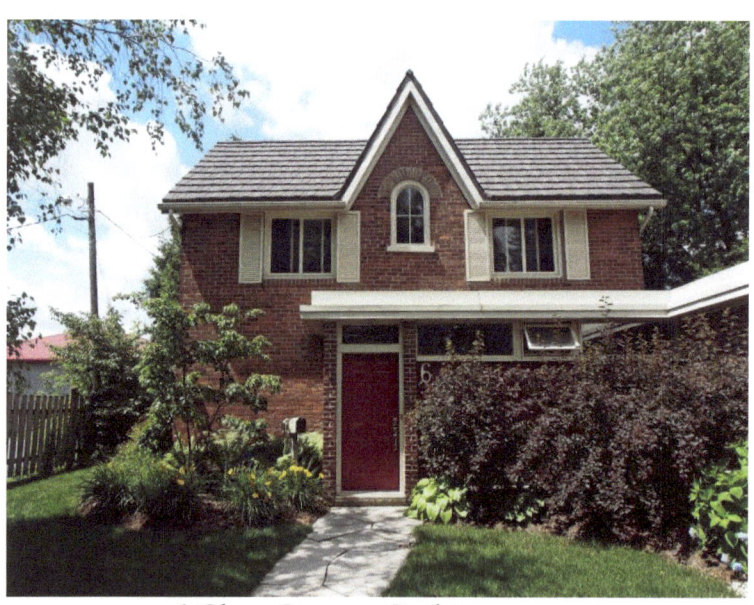

6 Clara Street - Gothic cottage

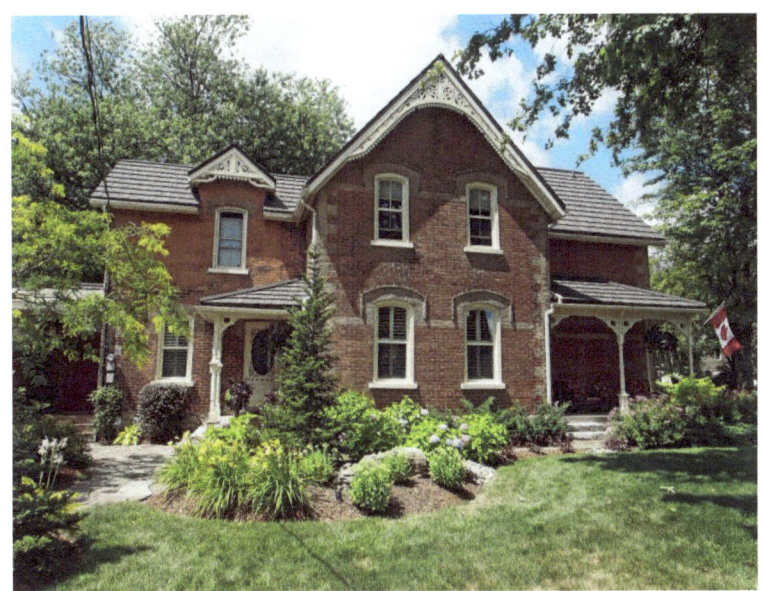

8 Clara Street – Gothic Revival – fancy bargeboard, dichromatic brickwork – Joseph Riddell, Veterinarian – 1883

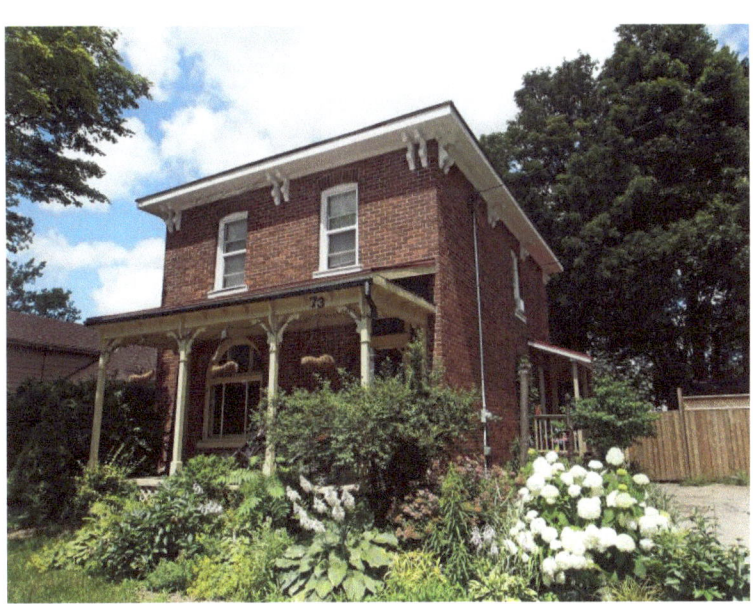

73 Clara Street – Italianate – paired cornice brackets

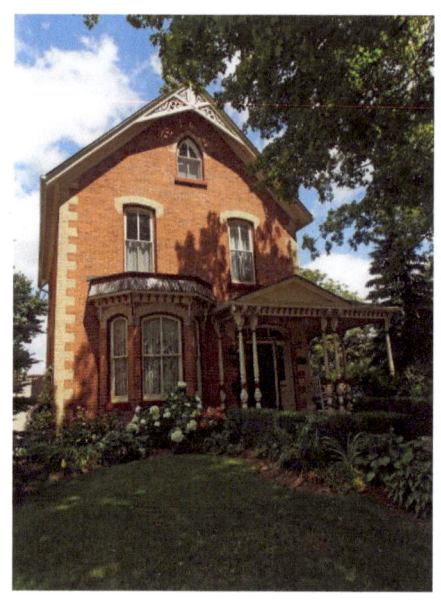

67 Clara Street – Gothic Revival – corner quoins

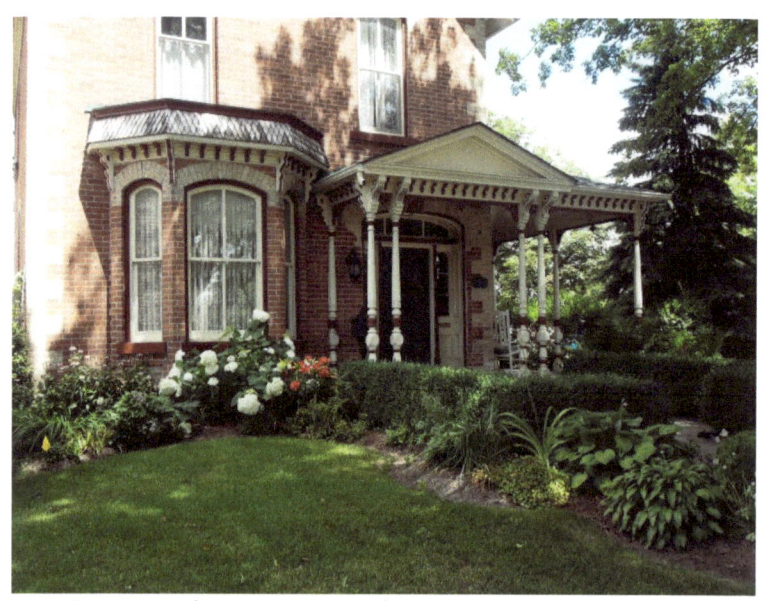

Bay window, narrow decorative porch pillars

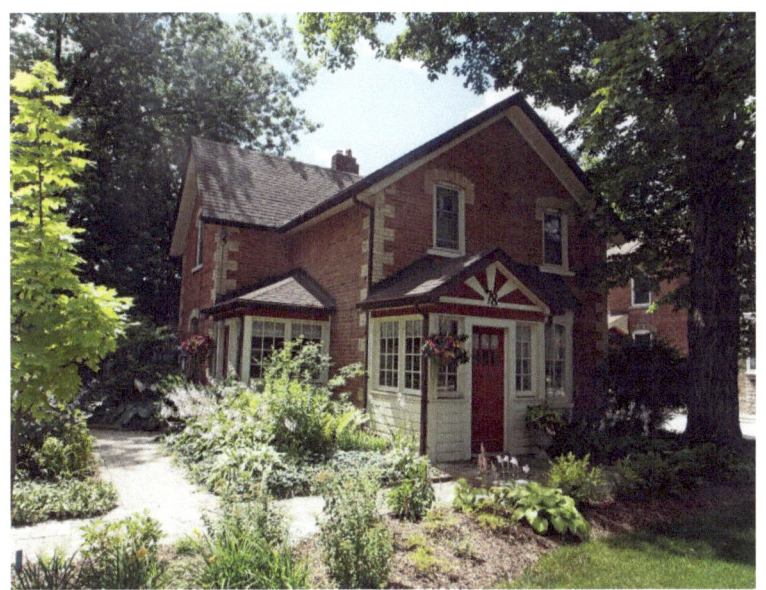

78 Clara Street – dichromatic brickwork,
buff coloured voussoirs

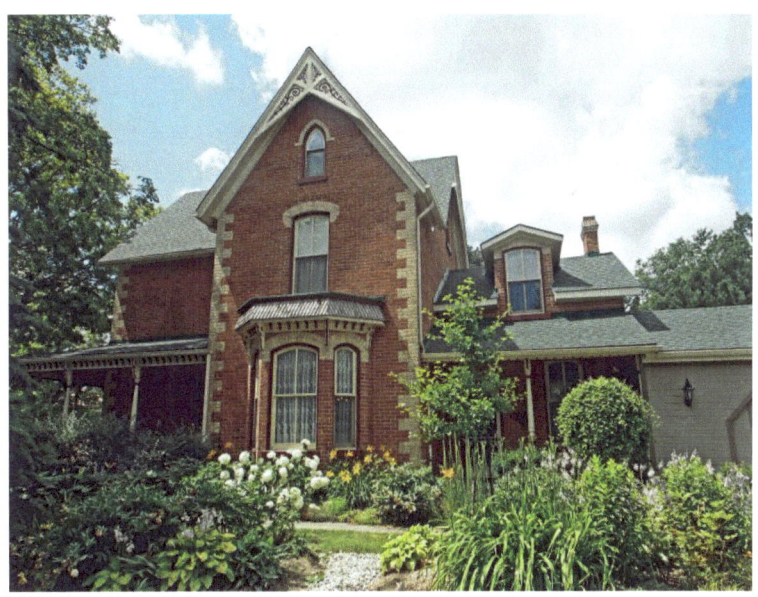

98 Clara Street – Gothic Revival – corner quoins

Elizabeth Street

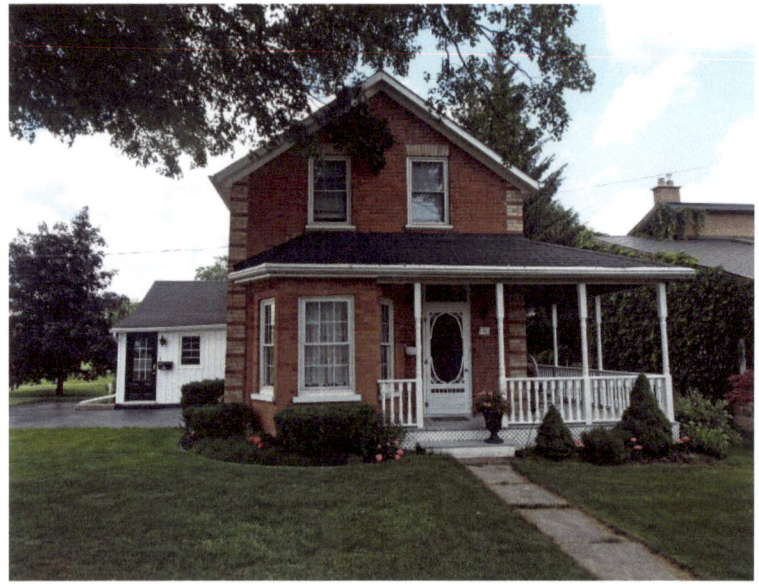

49 Elizabeth Street – Gothic Revival – corner quoins

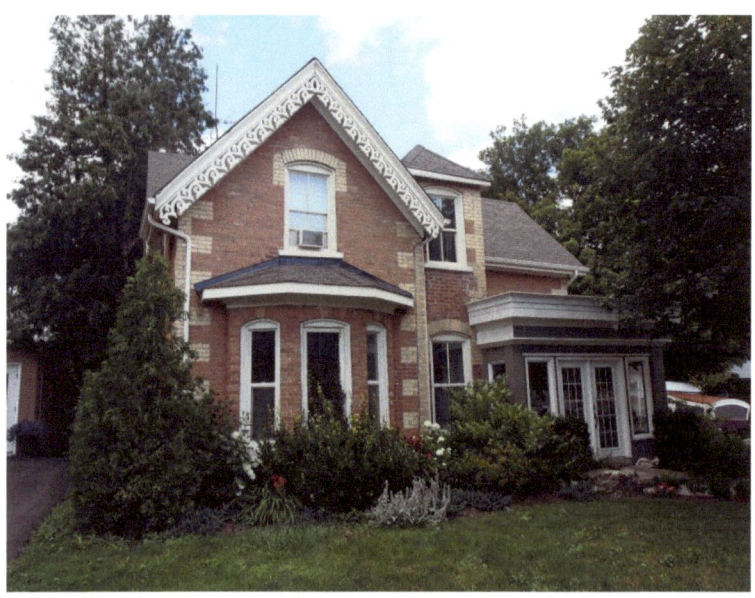

Gothic Revival – Vergeboard trim on gable, corner quoins

Second Street

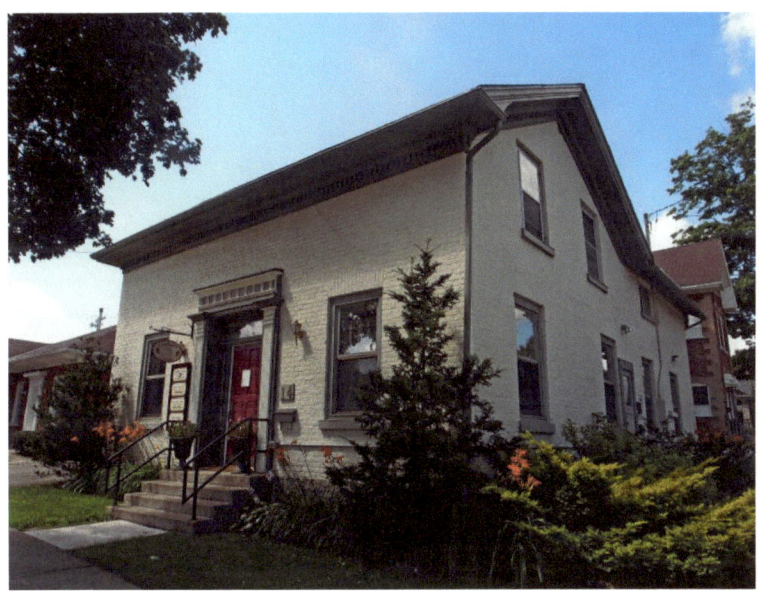

14 Second Street

Alexandra Park was named after Queen Alexandra consort of
King Edward VII who succeeded his mother Queen Victoria
in January 1901. The park, opened in August 1903, was built
on the site of the former town stockyards which held cattle
brought to the weekly market at the Town Hall. In 1923 the
Dufferin County War Memorial was constructed in the park.
The park originally wrapped around the Town Hall and out to
Broadway. In 1932 the Town sold off the Broadway footage
for a creamery and cold storage facility.

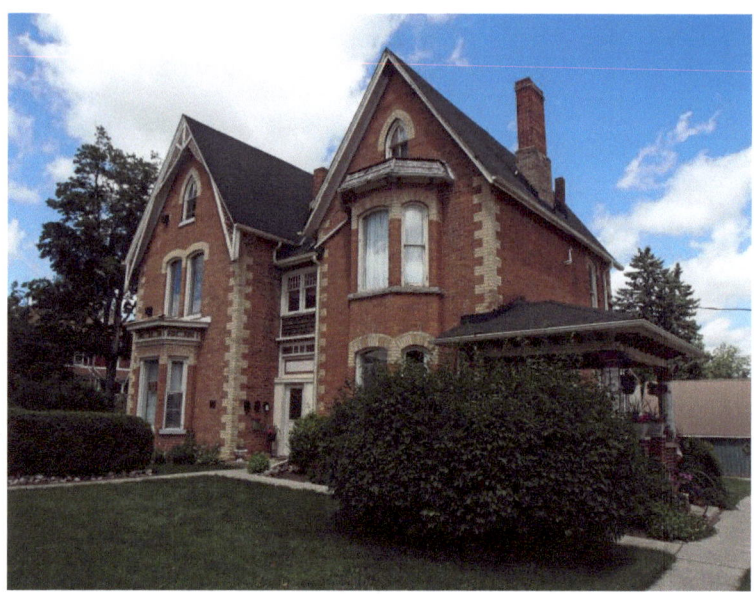

1 First Avenue – Gothic Revival – The John Green House built in 1875. Green owned a general store at Broadway and First Street, owned 111 acres with two houses, three shops, and two barns.

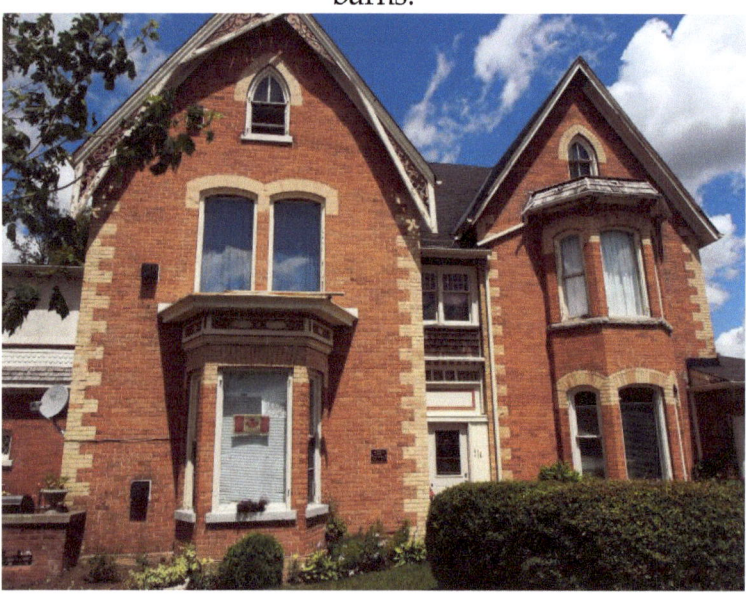

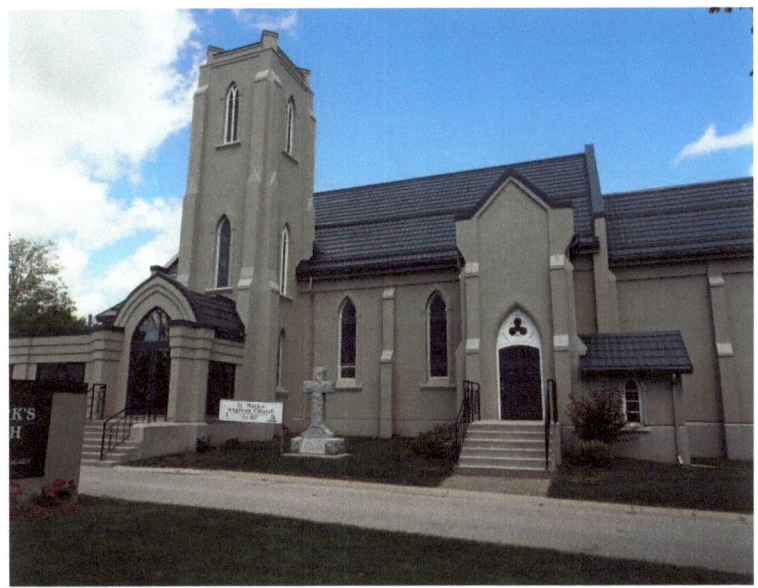

5 First Avenue – St. Mark's Anglican Church established in 1837 – the present church building was erected in 1868.

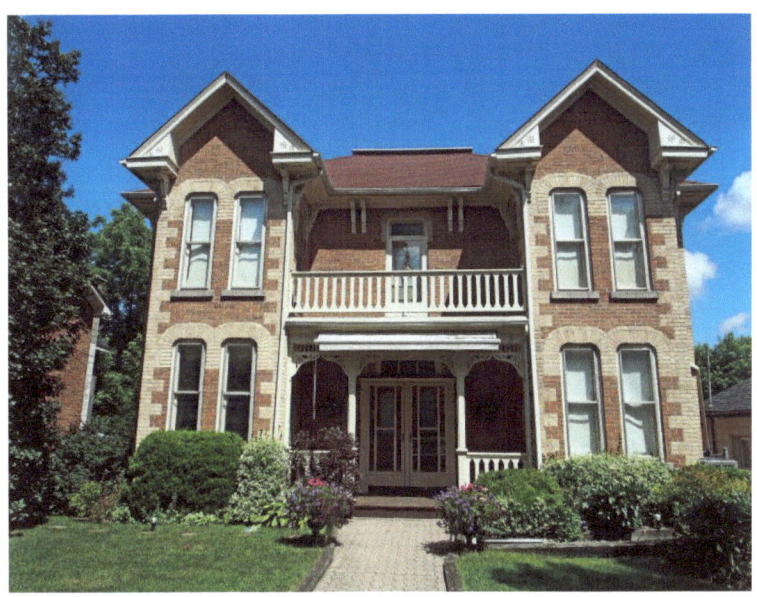

Gothic Revival – decorative dichromatic brickwork, paired cornice brackets, cornice return on the gables

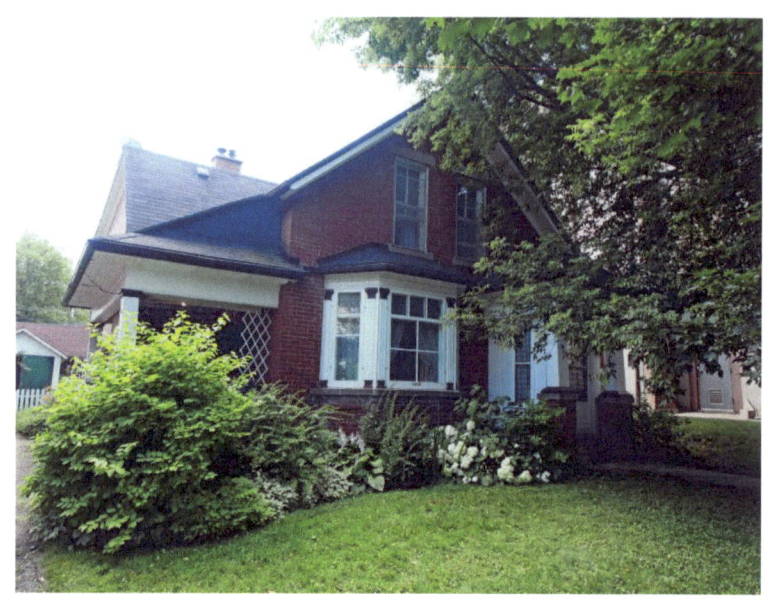

10 First Avenue with old livery behind it

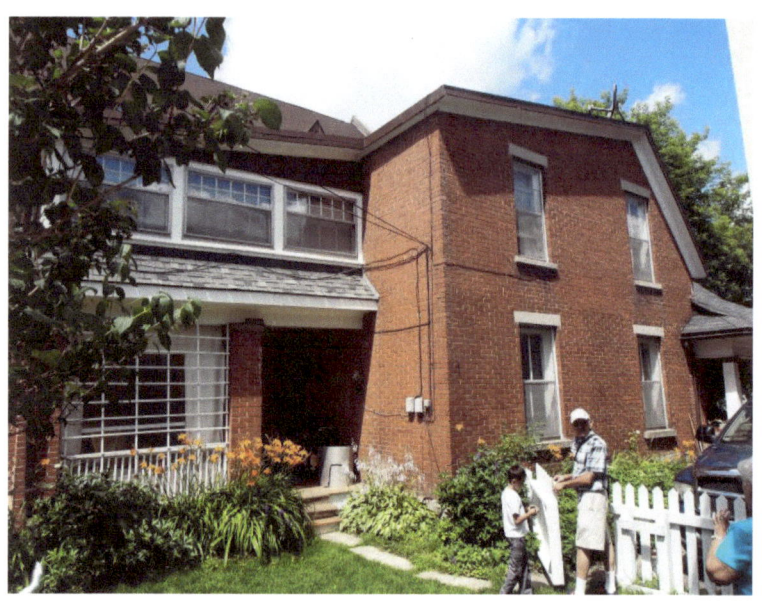

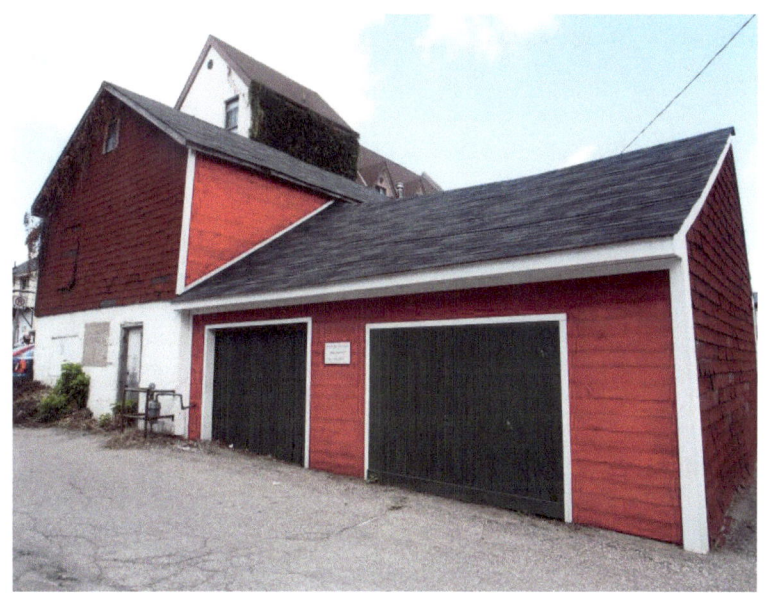

Old Livery Stable

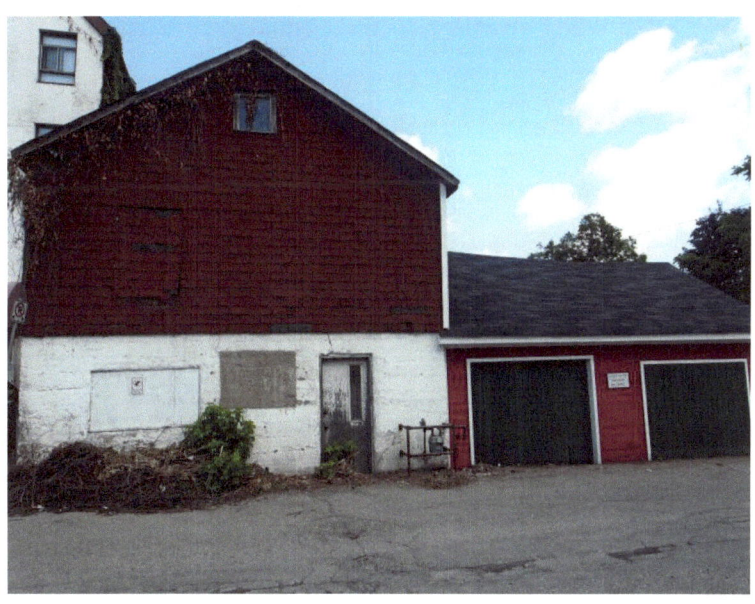

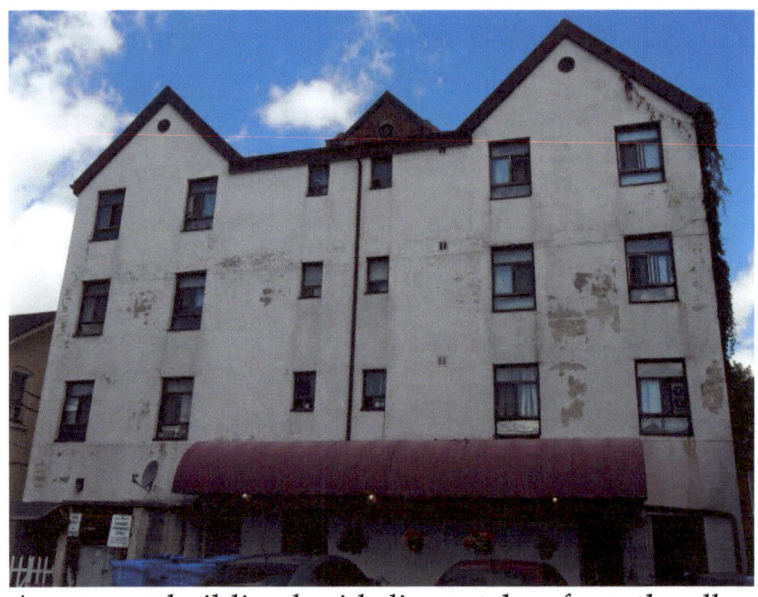

Apartment building beside livery taken from the alley

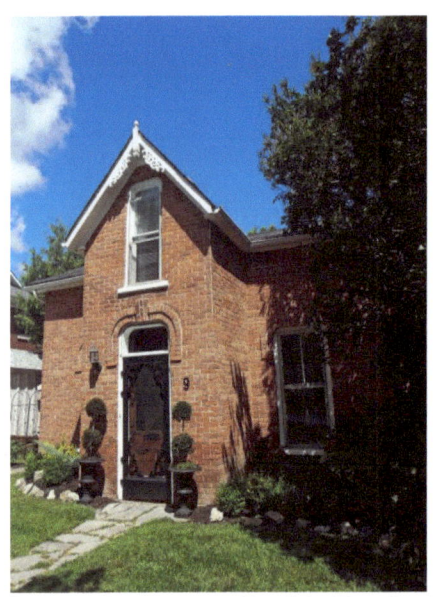

9 First Avenue – Gothic Revival – decorative bargeboard on the gable, decorative voussoir and keystone brickwork above the door

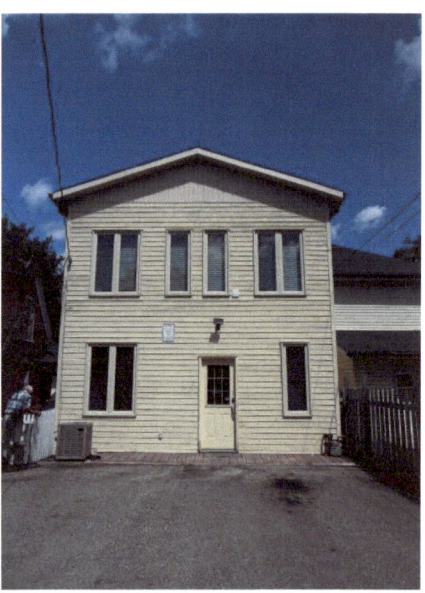

12 First Avenue from rear

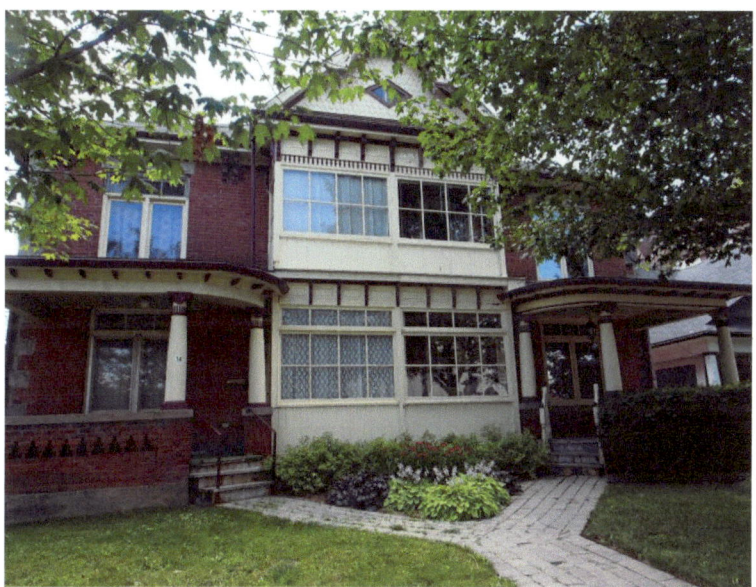

12-14 First Avenue – Gothic Revival – paired cornice brackets, verandahs

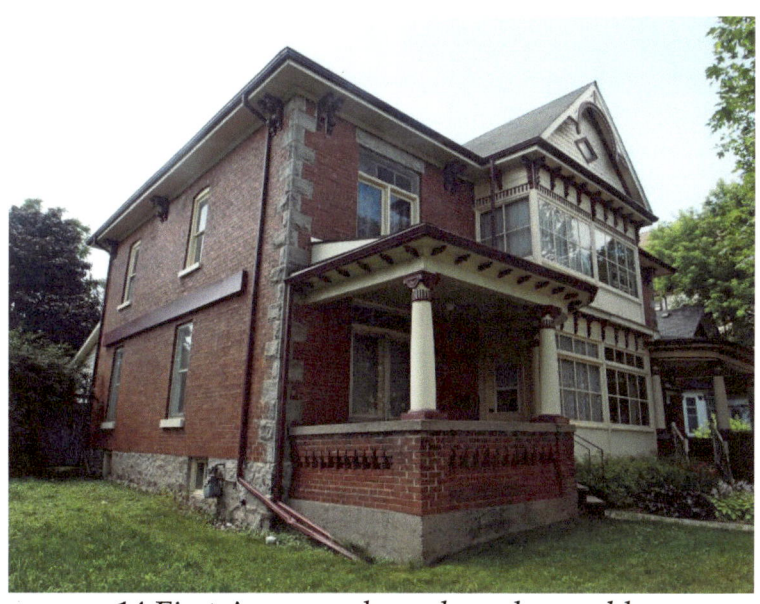

14 First Avenue – bargeboard on gable

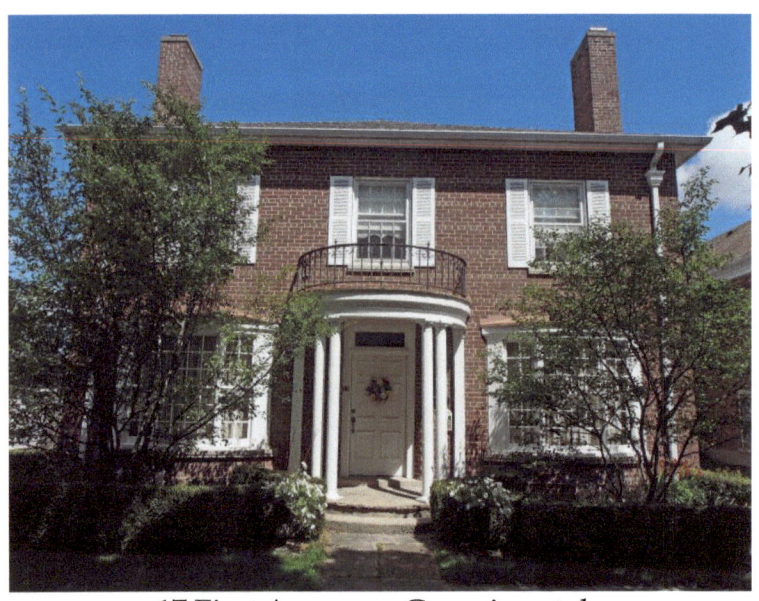

17 First Avenue – Georgian style

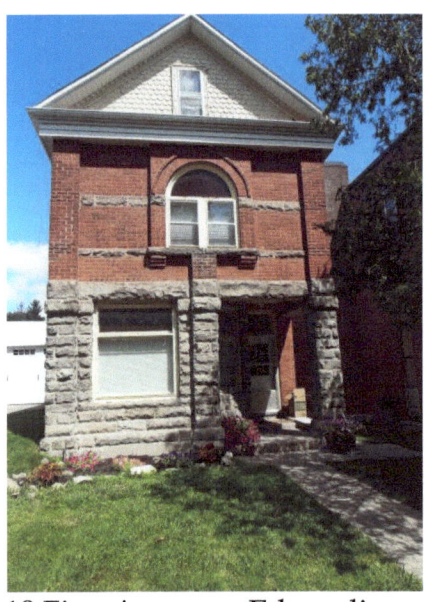

19 First Avenue – Edwardian
style – heavy cement banding

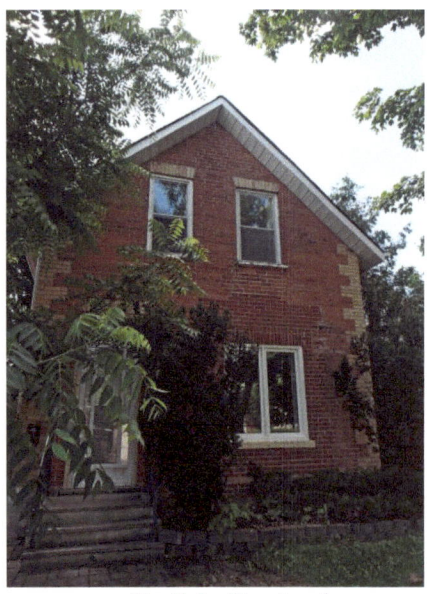

Gothic Revival
corner quoins

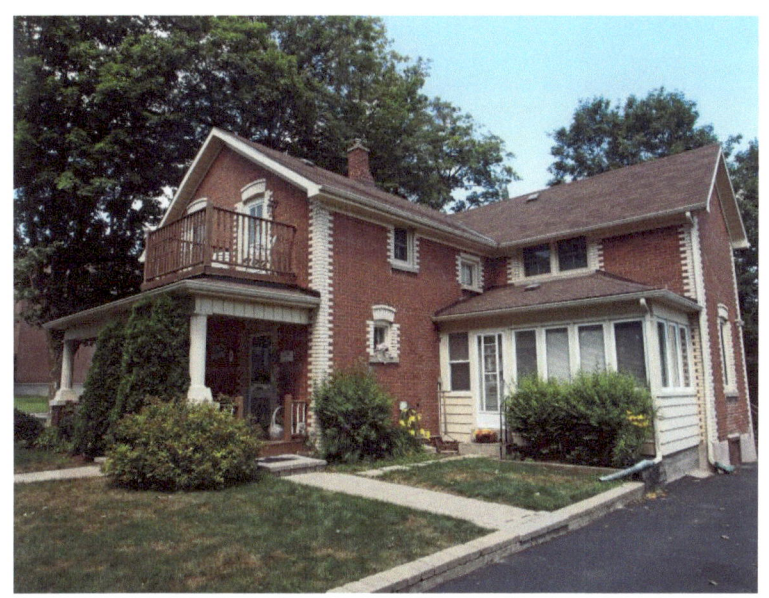

25 First Avenue – Gothic Revival
Robert Irvine, painter – c. 1885
Irvine House Bed and Breakfast

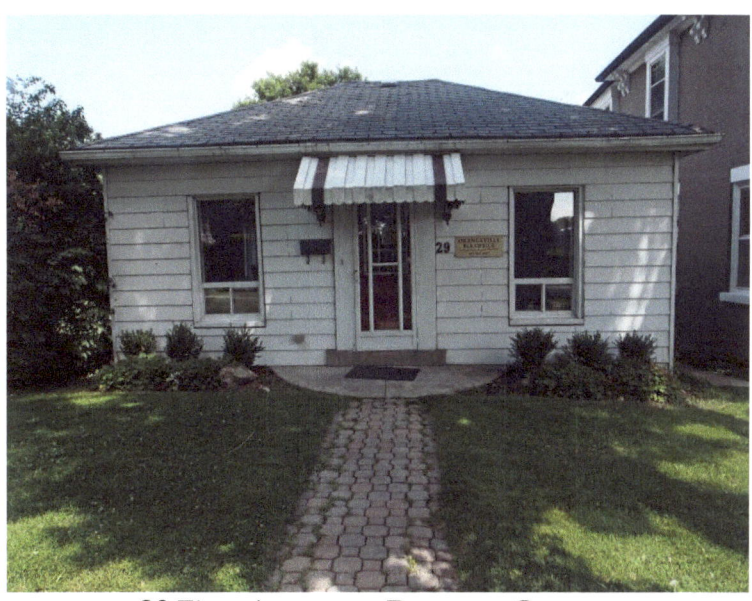

29 First Avenue – Regency Cottage
Orangeville BIA Office

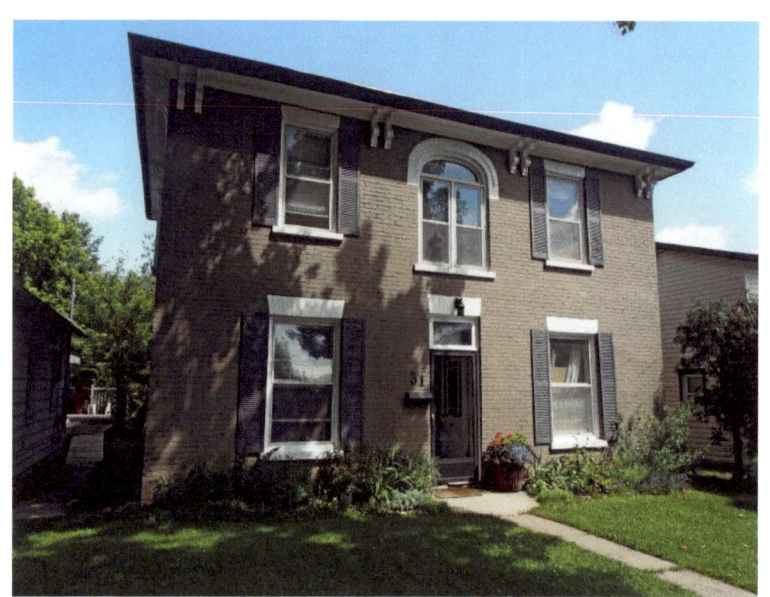

31 First Avenue

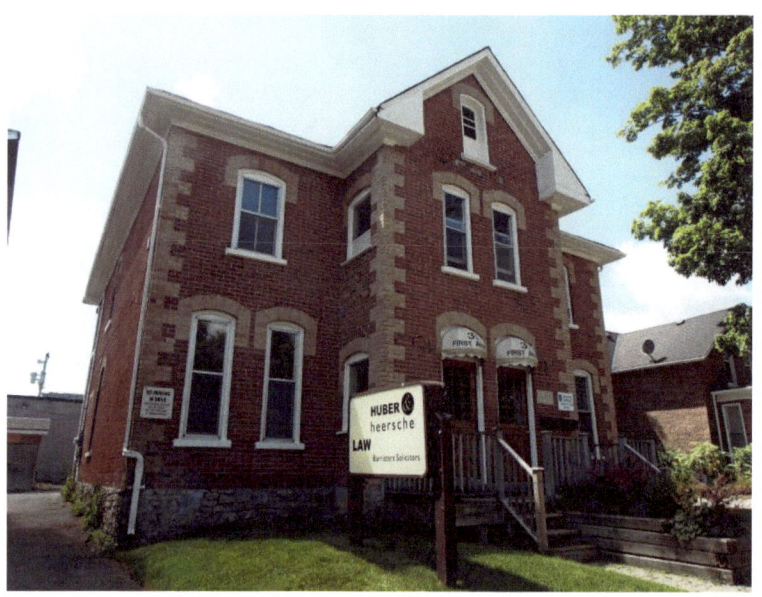

34 First Avenue – Gothic Revival

First Street

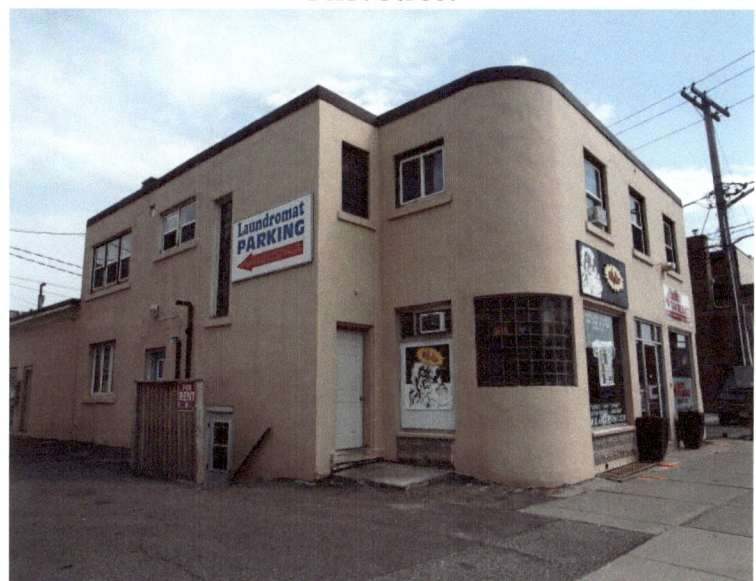

5 First Street – Art Moderne style with flat roof, glass block windows, curved corners – built by Fred Webb c. 1944 and housed the Orangeville Dairy and Dairy Bar until 1969

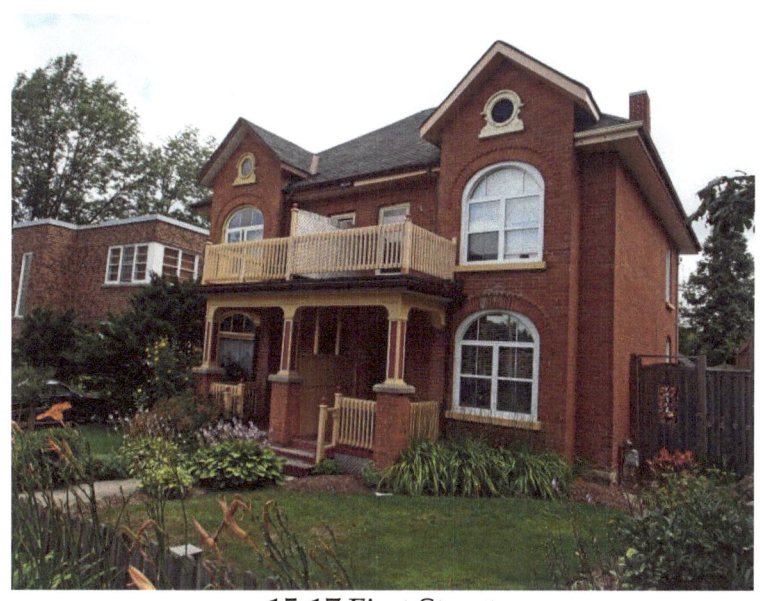

15-17 First Street

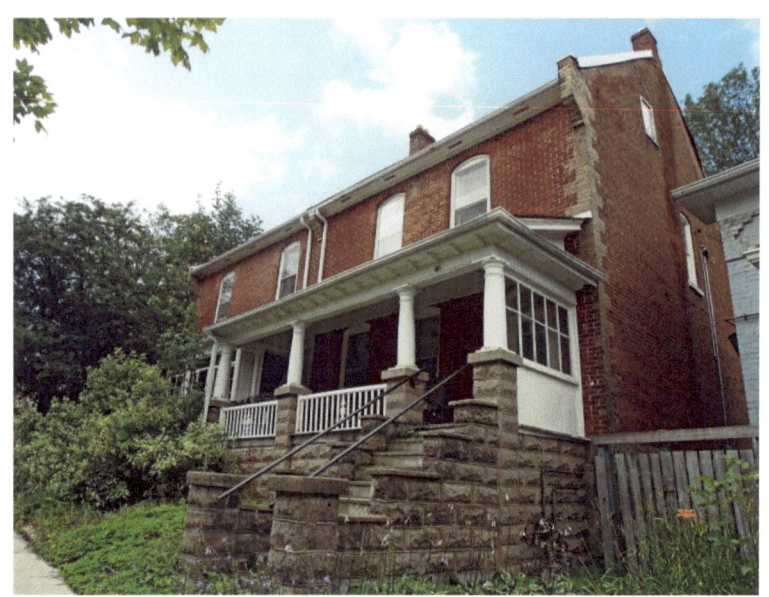

18 First Street

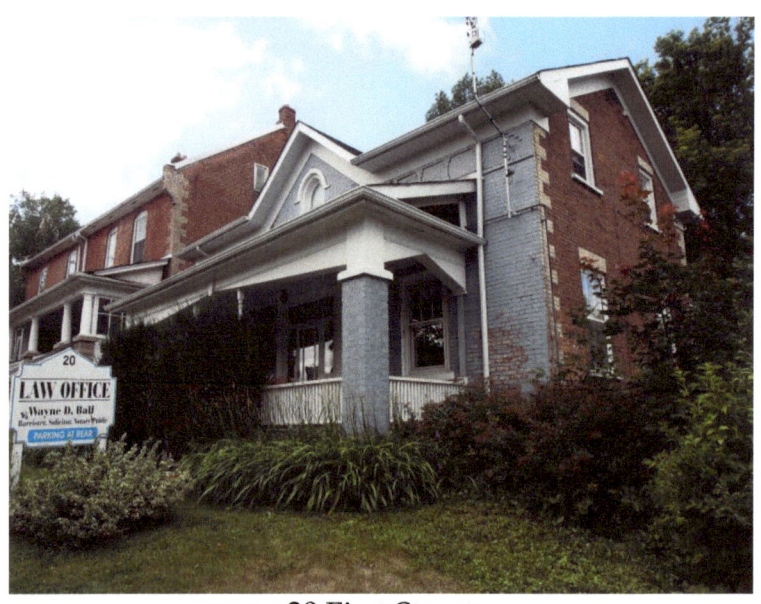

20 First Street

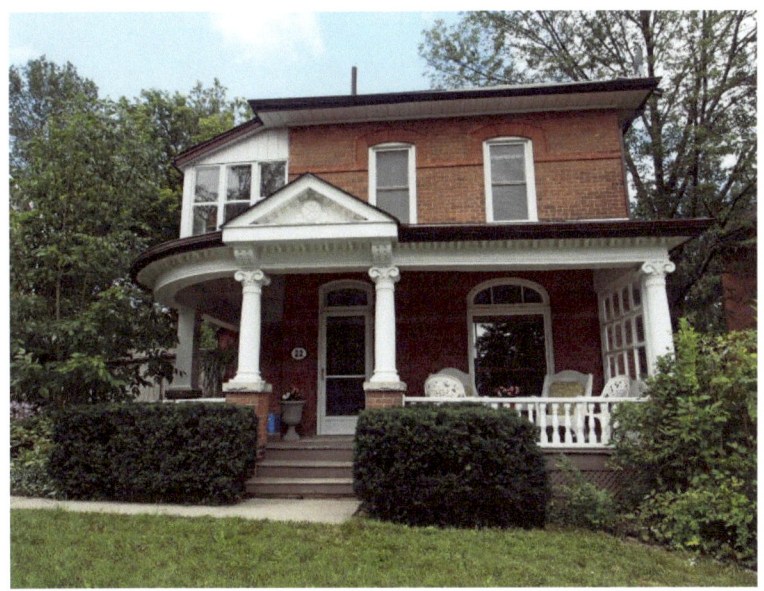

22 First Street – Italianate style with wide bracketed eaves, wrap-around verandah, triangular pediment with decorated tympanum

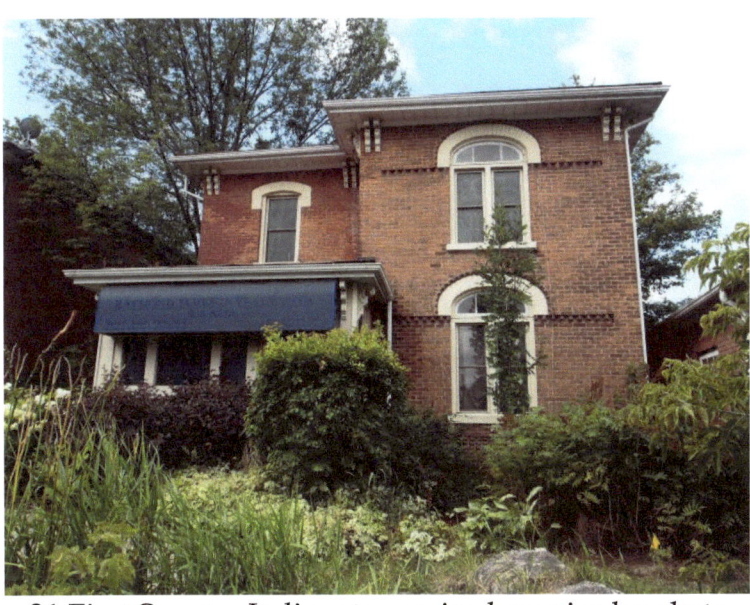

31 First Street – Italianate – paired cornice brackets

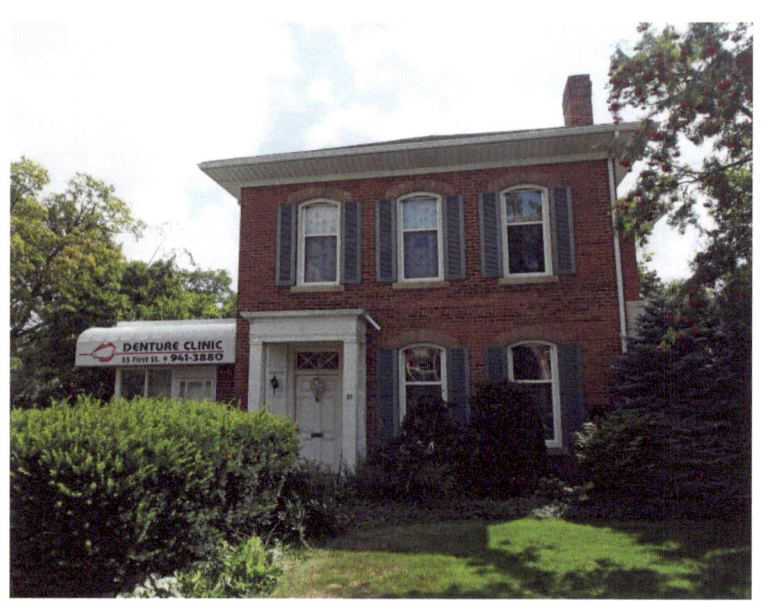

33 First Street – modified Georgian style

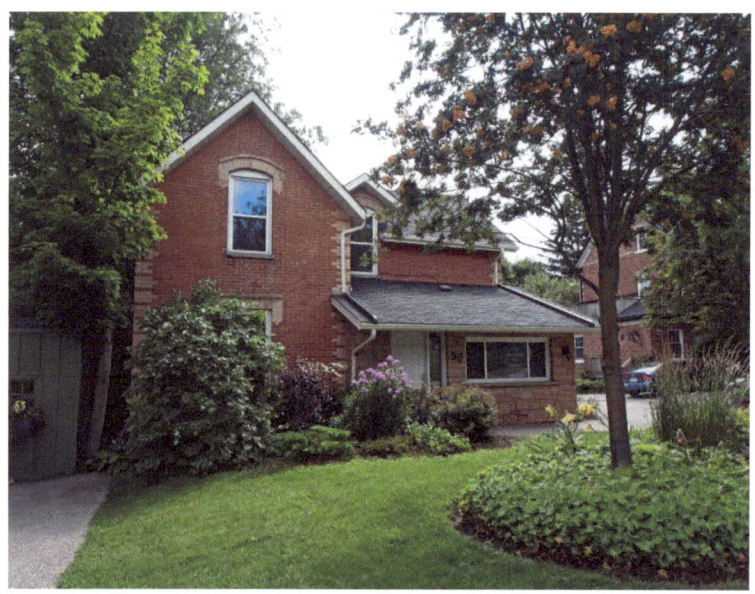

39 First Street – Gothic Revival – corner quoins

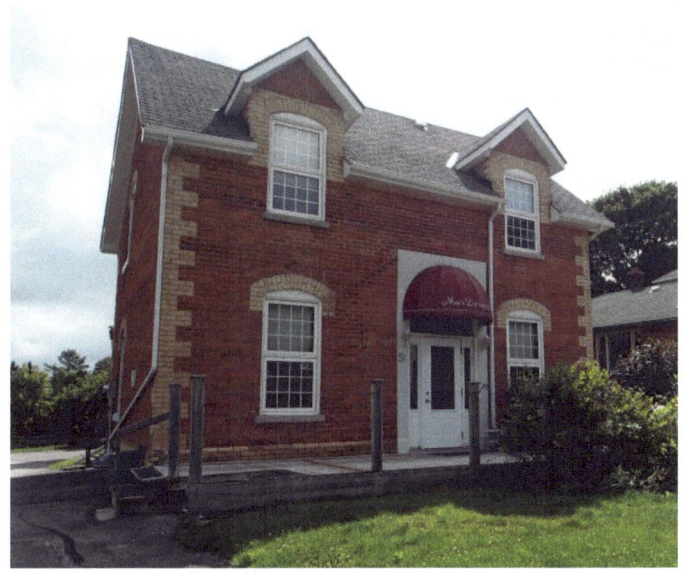

51 First Street – Italianate style

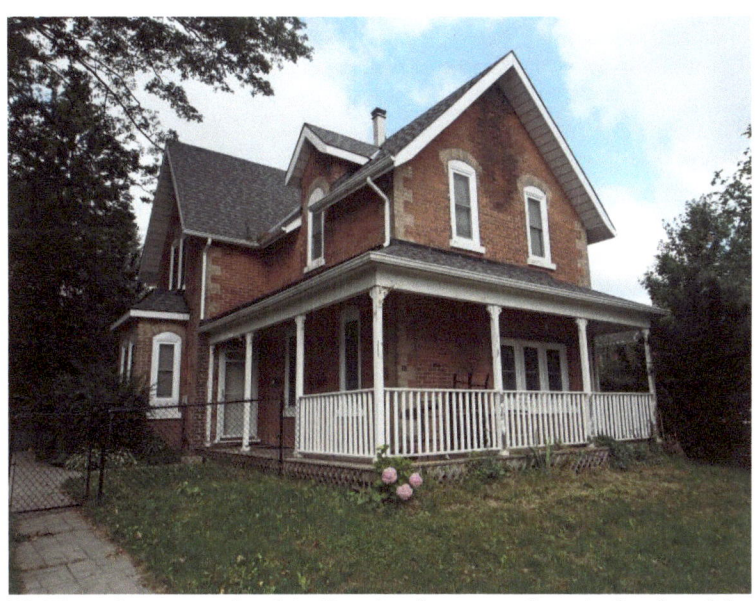

50 First Street – Gothic Revival – steeply pitched gable, dichromatic brickwork

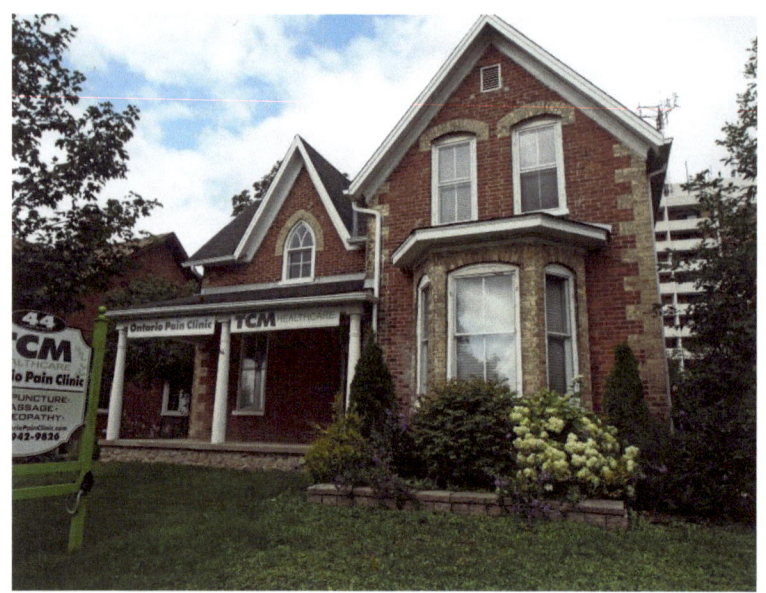

44 First Street – Gothic Revival with lighter-coloured decorative brickwork, corner quoins, brick voussoirs

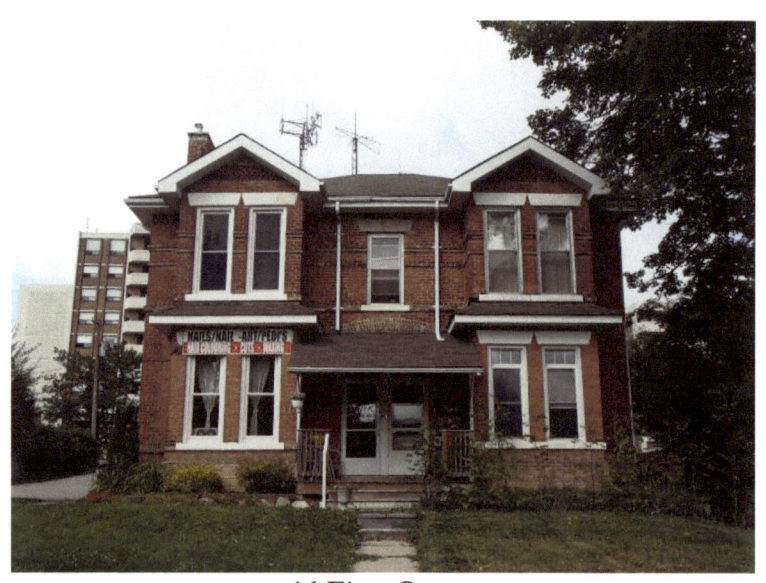

46 First Street

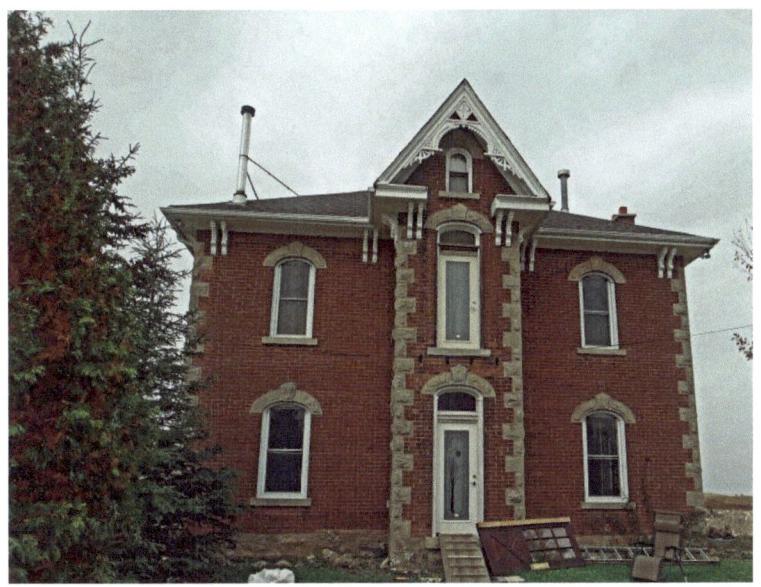

1st Line and Highway 9 – Romanesque style – decorative vergeboard on gable, paired cornice brackets, quoining on centre tower and corners, rounded window vouissors with keystones

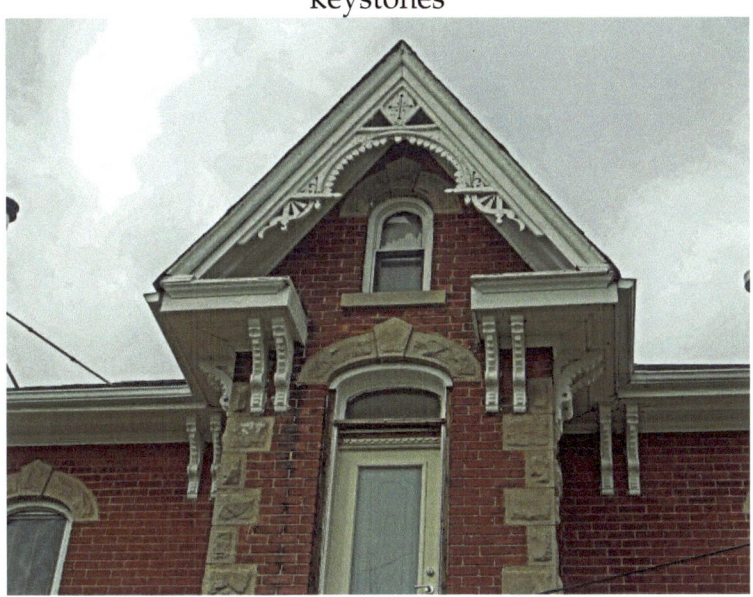

Cornice return on gable ends

Sculptures in Orangeville

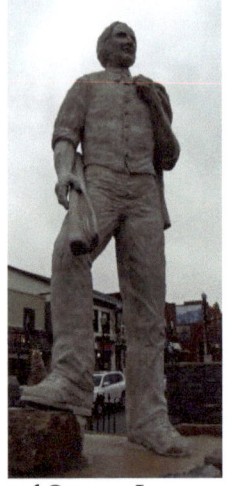

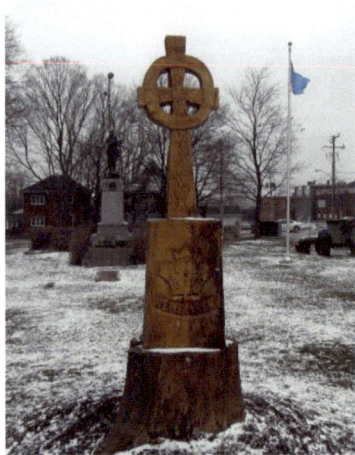

Statue of Orange Lawrence
Founder 1796-1861

Remembrance Carving in
Alexandra Park

The first tree was carved in 2003. The sculptures are about art and community. Carvers create animals, historical figures, men, women, and tree spirits.

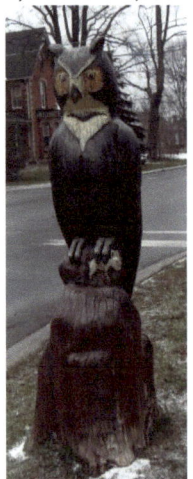

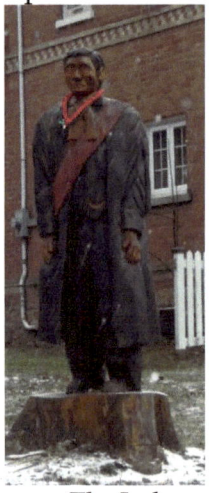

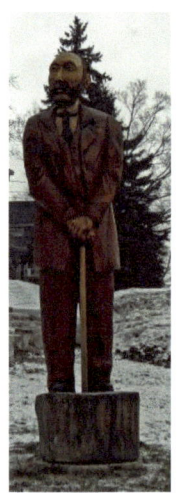

Great Horned Owl
Clara at Zina Street
Artist Tim Braithwaite

The Judge
62 Zina Street

The Prince of Wales
First and Zina Streets

Artist Jim Menken

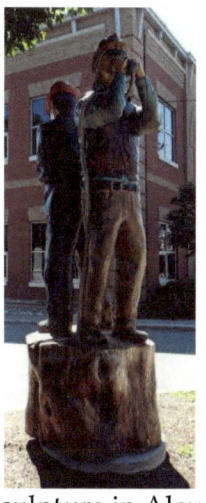
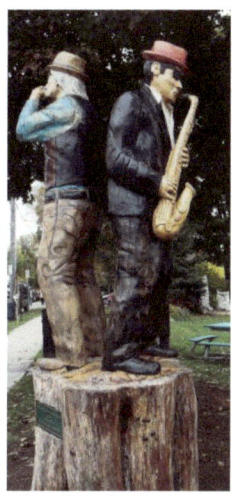

The Musicians sculpture in Alexandra Park (just north of the Town Hall) is a tribute to the 10th anniversary of the Orangeville Blues and Jazz Festival in 2012. On musician is playing a harmonica (Blues) and the second musician is playing a saxophone (Jazz). Created by local artist Jim Menken.

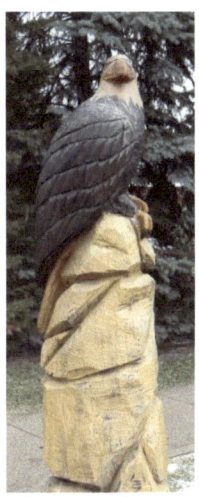
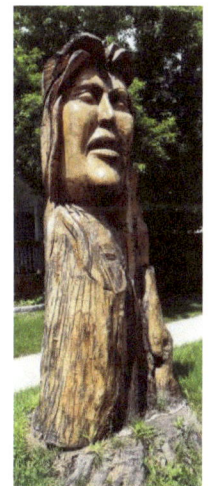
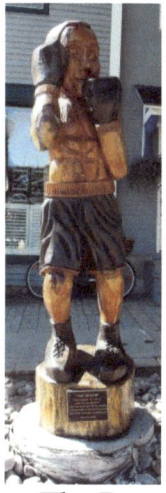

The Eagle
Clara St. near Zina
Artist Jim Menken

The Lady
4 Clara Street
Artist Paul Frenette

The Boxer
64 Broadway

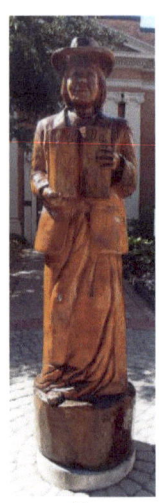

The Storyteller at library

Marilyn Harding Doekes was an elementary school teacher and Resource Librarian for over 30 years. She enjoyed sharing stories with the children and was in demand as a "storyteller" at school, at church, in people's homes and at community events. Artist Jim Menken in 2006

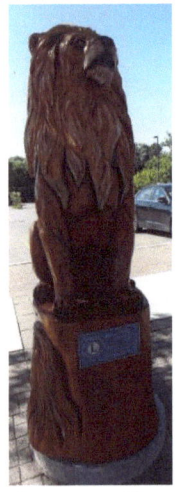 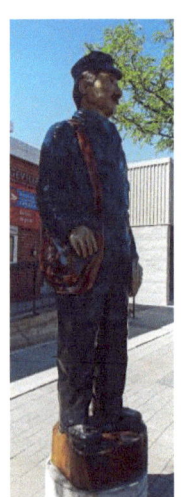 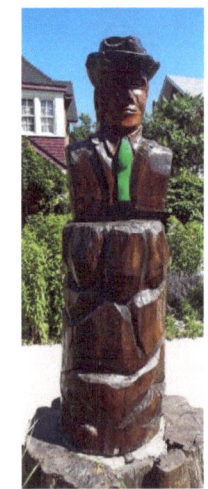

Amaranth   Letter Carrier   Alexander Dunlop McKitrick
Lions Club   216 Broadway   255 Broadway
                  Artist Jim Menken   Artist Peter Mogensen

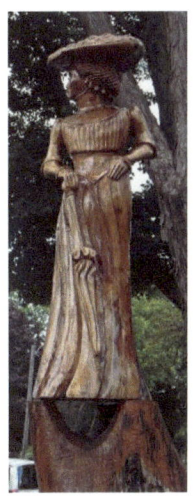
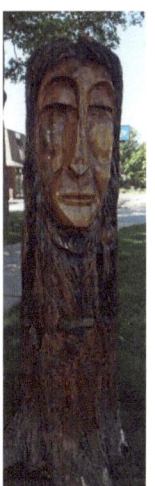
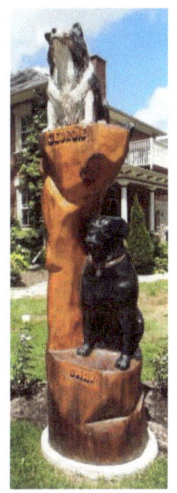

Victorian Lady
7 Zina Street
Artist Robbin Wenzoski

The Indian
255 Broadway
Jeff Waters

Tribute to Dogs
65 Zina Street
Jim Menken

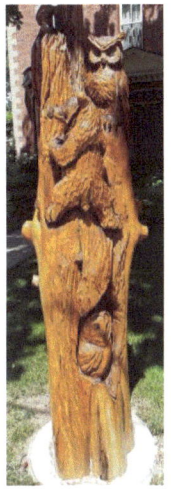
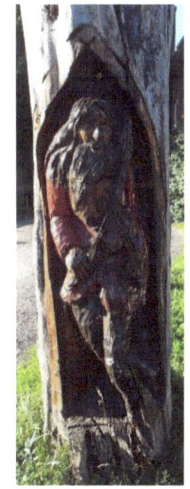
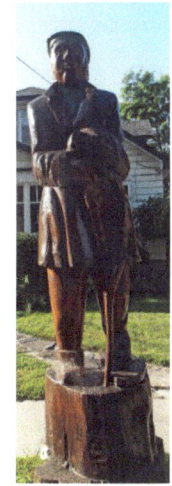

Canadian Nature
-a bear, woodpecker,
two owls

The Fiddler
257 Broadway
Artist Nick Onac

Dr.A.G.Campbell
21 York Street
Artist Peter Mogensen

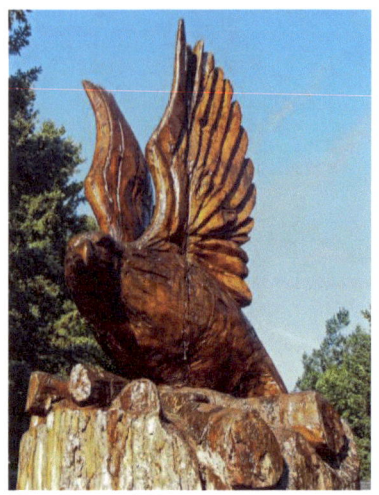

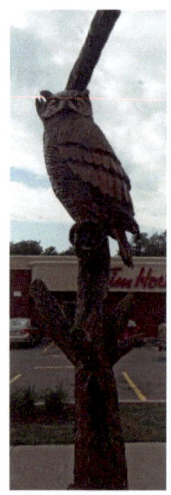

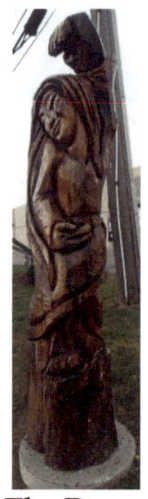

Eagle on Nest
60 Mill Street
Artist Peter Turrell

Owl in Tree
61 Broadway
Artist Rob McFaul

The Dancer
40 Broadway
Bobbi Switzer

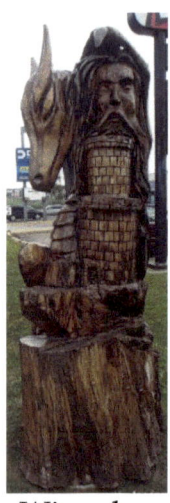

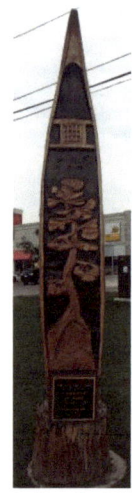

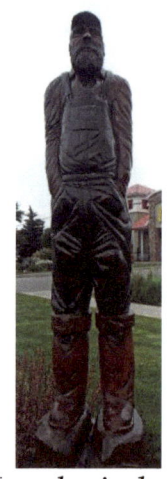

The Wizard
and Dragon
38 Broadway
Artist Paul Frenette

Canoe & Jack Pine
25 Broadway
Artist Nick Hall

Lumberjack
Broadway
across from
McDonald's

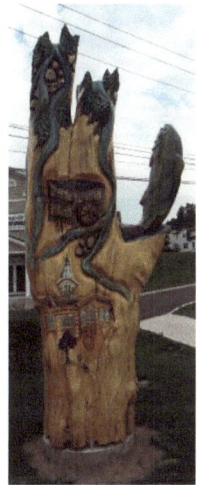
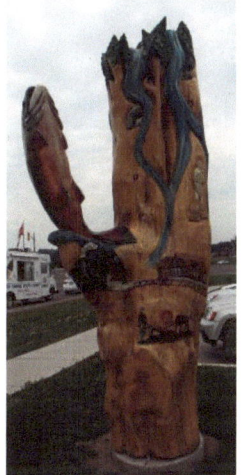

New carving at the Information Centre

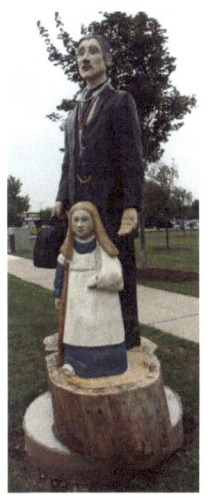
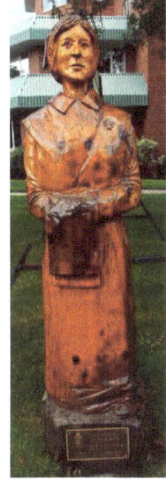
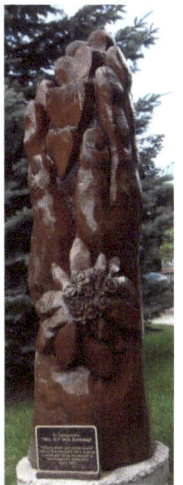

Physician and Patient
100 Rolling Hills Drive (Hospital)
Artist Jim Menken

The Nurse
IODE's 100th anniversary in 2007 – sits in front of former Hospital 32 First St
Artist Jim Menken

Helping Hands & Caring Hearts
Elizabeth Street
Mrs. Baniulis spent many years as nurse and caring for seniors

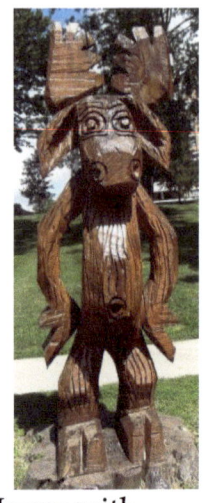
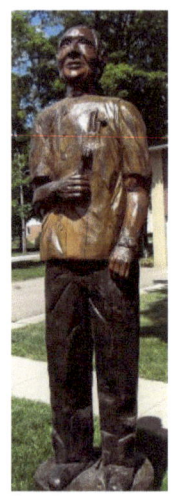
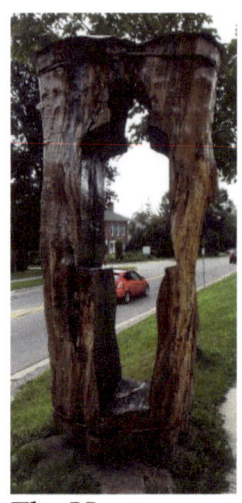

Moose with
Attitude
McCarthy St.
Artist Bob DeVries

The Dentist
19 McCarthy St.
outside home of
Dentist John Russell
Artist Jim Menken

The Hunter
48 First Street
Artist Don Miller

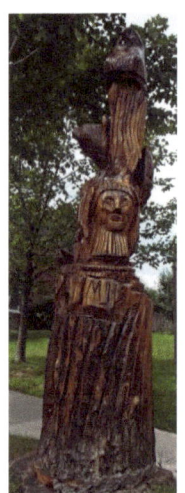

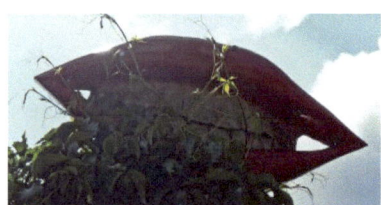

Canadian Fighting Spirits
(dedicated to Canadian troops
in Afghanistan) 48 First St.
Artist Murray Berger

The Smile
33 First Street
Artist Robbin Wenzoski

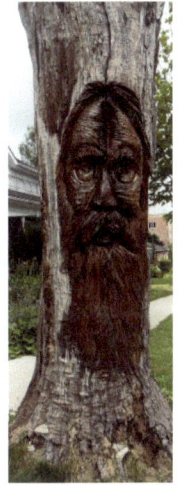
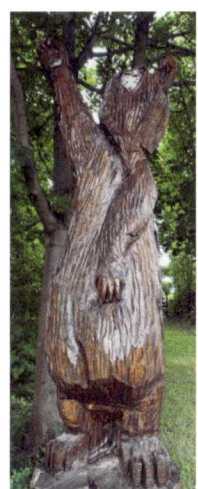
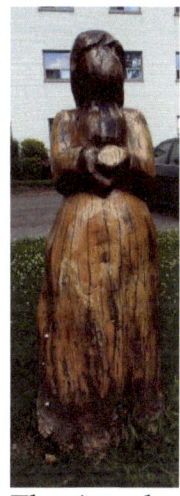

Tree Spirit   Waving Bear   The Angel
267 Broadway   11 First Street   9 McCarthy St.
Artist Colin Partridge   Artist Walter vanderWindt

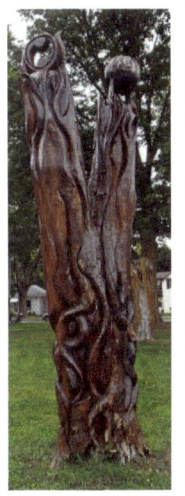
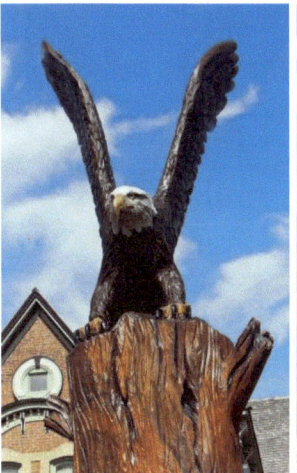
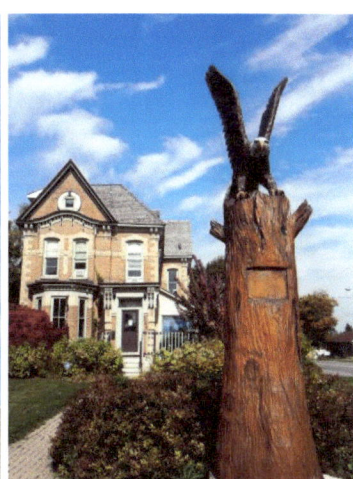

Carving at   Eagle at 299 Broadway
Alexandra Park

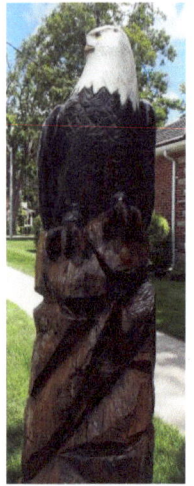

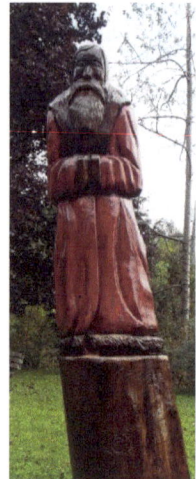

Eagle   Kris Kringle

Caledon Village

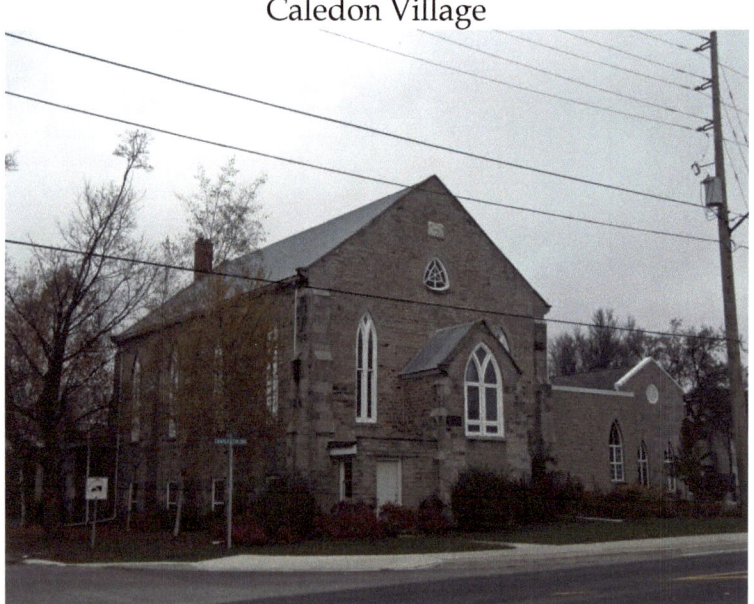

Knox United Church – A.D. 1873

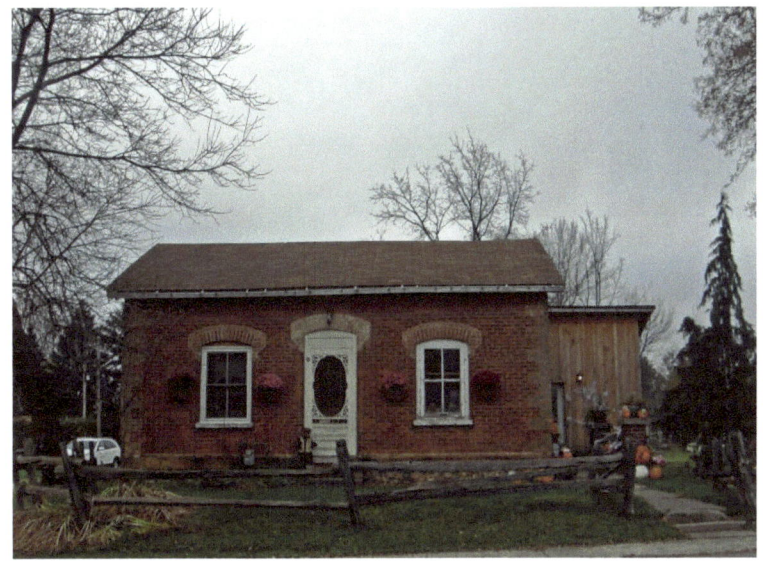

Regency Cottage in red brick with quoining on the corners, buff coloured voussoirs

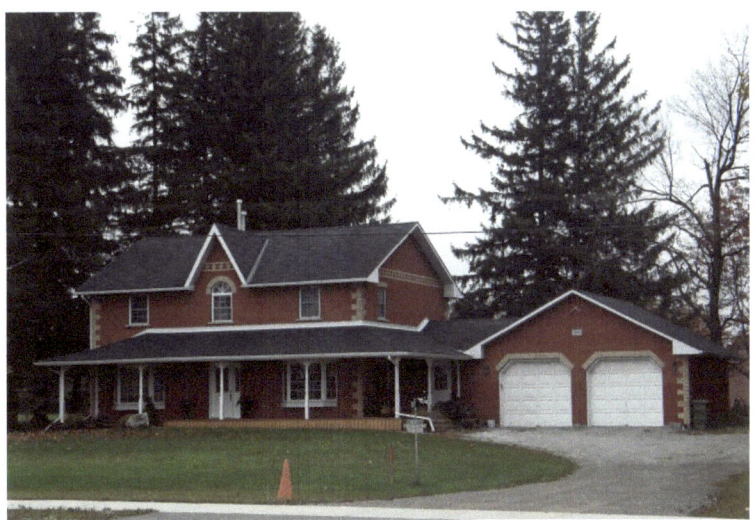

Buff coloured banding and on corners and voussoirs

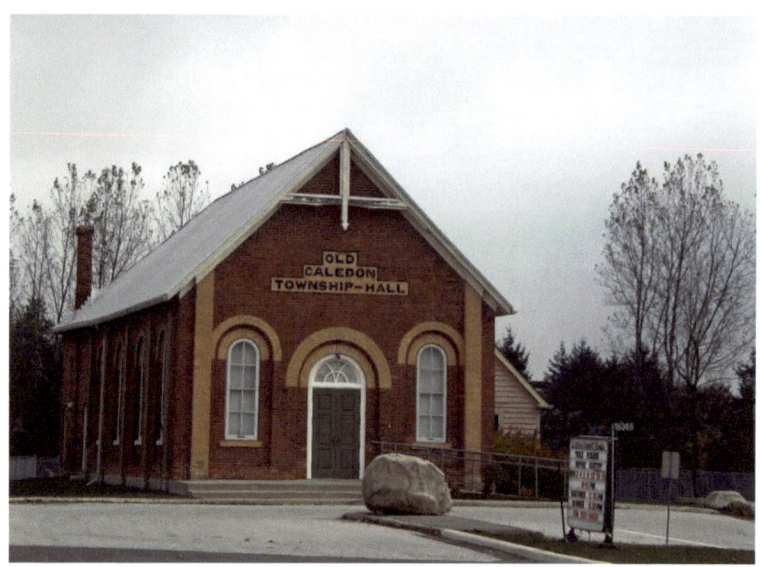

Old Caledon Township Hall – A.D. 1875 – used as a court house, hall, library, now a theatre for Caledown Town Hall Players. The rectangular, gable-roofed building, with its red brick construction, decorative buff brick detailing and rounded multi-pane windows, shows municipal architecture of the 1870s.

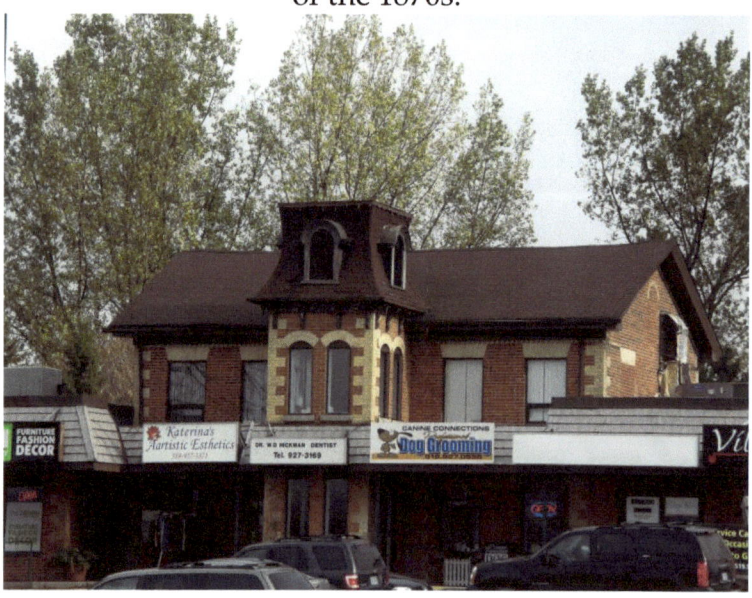

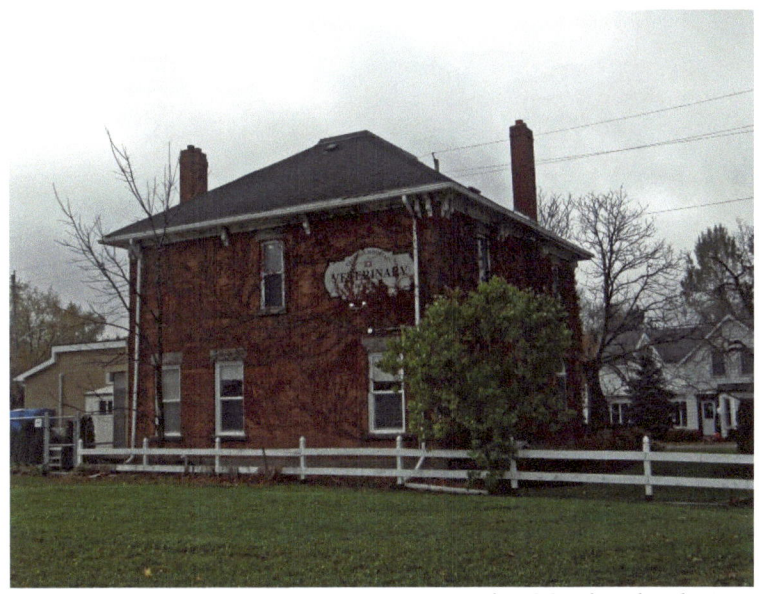

Caledon Mountain Veterinary Hospital – 29 Elizabeth Street – Italianate with single cornice brackets (double at corners), heavy stone window lintels

Mono Centre

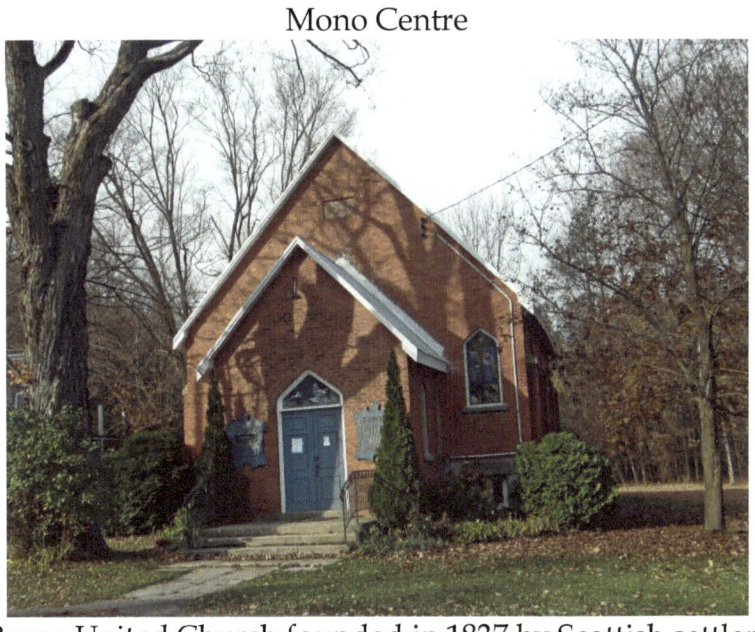

Burns United Church founded in 1837 by Scottish settlers

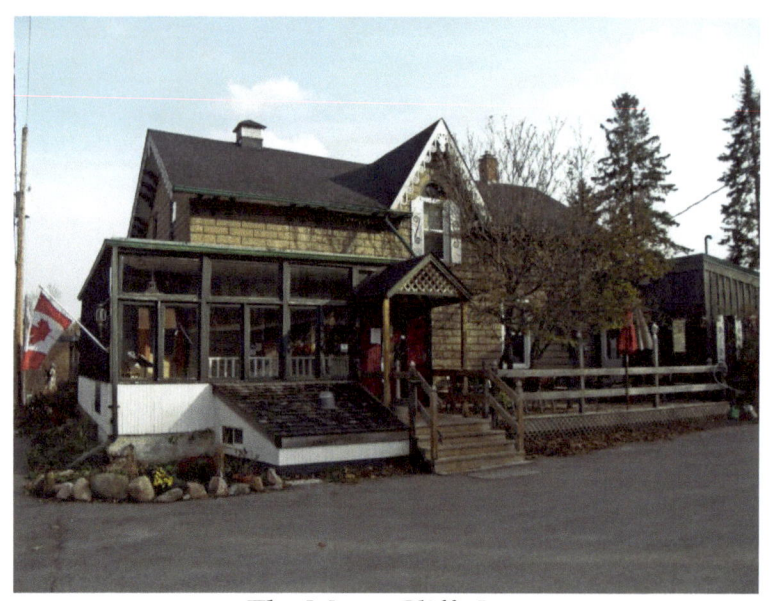

The Mono Cliffs Inn

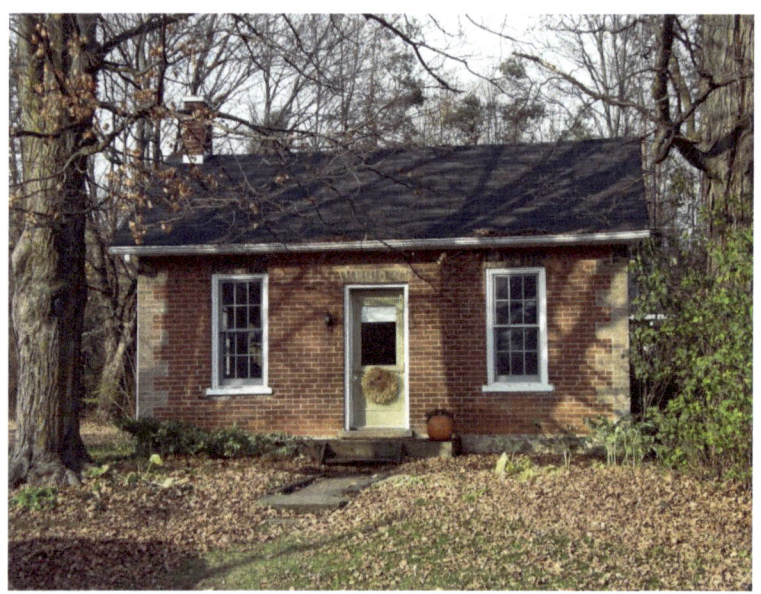

Regency Cottage – buff coloured quoining at the corners

Architectural Terms

Belvedere: (from the Italian "beautiful view") an architectural feature on a roof, in a garden or on a terrace that gives a beautiful view. Example: 28 Zina Street	
Brackets: a decorative or weight-bearing structural element which forms a right angle with one side against a wall and the other under a projecting surface such as an eave or roof. Example: 63 Zina Street	
Buttress: a masonry structure built against or projecting from a wall which serves to support or reinforce the wall. In Canadian architecture, they are sometimes used for decoration. Example: 3 Zina Street	
Cornice: originally the wooden overhang of the roof. With the use of stone, brick, iron and steel, the cornice is any projecting shelf at the top of a ceiling or roof. They can be very decorative. Example: 51 Zina Street	
Dentil Moulding: an even series of rectangles used as ornamental decoration in cornices. Example: 64 Zina Street	

Dichromatic brickwork: the use of two colours of brick, tile or slate to decorate a façade. Example: 51 Zina Street	
Dormer: (French for "sleep") a gable end window that pierces through the plane of a sloping roof surface to create usable space in the top floor or attic of a building by adding headroom. Example: 17 Zina Street	
Finial: ornament added to the top of a gable, pinnacle, canopy or spire – a Gothic element. Example: 41 Zina Street	
Fretwork: interlaced decorative design resembling a bracket Example: 2-6 Zina Street	
Gable: the triangular portion of a wall between the edges of a sloping roof. Example: 11 Zina Street	

Hipped Roof: a roof where all sides slope downwards to the walls with no gables. Example: Caledon Mountain Veterinary Hospital, 29 Elizabeth Street, Caledon Village	
Keystones and Voussoirs: a voussoir is a wedge-shaped element used in building an arch. A keystone is the central stone that locks all the stones into position, allowing the arch to bear weight. A keystone is often enlarged and embellished. Example: 62 Zina Street	
Lancet Window: a tall, narrow window with a pointed arch at its top. Example: 3 Zina Street	
Palladian Window: a large window that is divided into three sections with the centre section larger than the two side sections and usually arched. Example: 27 Zina Street	
Pediment: a triangular section above the horizontal structure (entablature), typically supported by columns. The inside of the triangle is called the tympanum. Example: 51 Zina Street	
Quoin: masonry blocks at the corner of a wall, often a decorative feature, usually larger or of a different colour than the rest of the wall. Example: Clara Street	

Rose Window: a circular window with ornamental tracery radiating from the centre. Example: 3 Zina Street	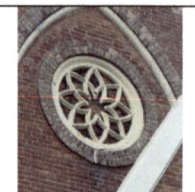
Sidelight: a window, usually with a vertical emphasis, that flanks a door, and is often used to emphasize the importance of a primary entrance. Example: 14 Second Street	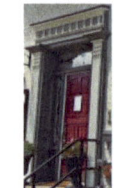
Vergeboards: also called bargeboards – hang from the projecting end of a roof and are often elaborately carved and ornamented. Example: 41 Zina Street	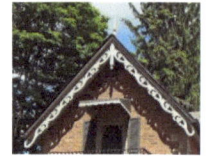

Orangeville's Building Styles

Art Moderne, 1930-1945 – This style originated in the United States with rounded corners, smooth walls, and flat roofs. Large expanses of glass were used, even wrapping around corners. Example: former Orangeville Dairy, 5 First Street	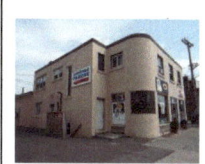
Edwardian, 1900-1930 – This style bridges the ornate and elaborate styles of the Victorian era and the simplified styles of the 20th century. Balanced facades, simple roof lines, dormer windows, large front porches, and smooth brick surfaces are its characteristics. Example: 24 Zina Street	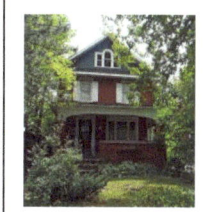
Georgian, before 1860 – This style began with the British King Georges in the 18th century. These buildings have balanced facades around a central door, medium-pitched gable roofs, and small paned windows. Example: 17 First Avenue	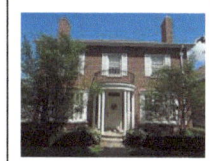
Gothic Revival, 1830-1890 – These decorative buildings have sharply-pitched gables with highly detailed vergeboards, pointed-arch window openings, and dichromatic brickwork. It is a common style in Ontario. Examples: 67 Zina Street	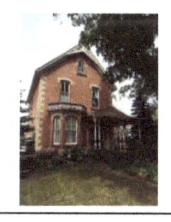

Italianate, 1850-1900 – It has wide-bracketed eaves, belvederes, wrap-around verandahs. Examples: 62 Zina Street	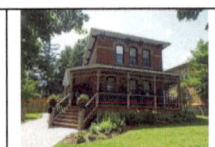
Regency Cottage, 1830-1860 – This style originated in England in 1815 and spread to Ontario later in the 19th century as British officers retired to Canada. It is a modest one-storey house with a low-pitched hip roof and has a symmetrical front façade. Example: 29 First Avenue	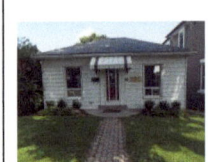
Romanesque Revival, 1880-1910 – This style hearkens back to medieval architecture of the 11th and 12th centuries with a heavy appearance, blocky towers and rounded arches. Example: 1st Line and Highway 9	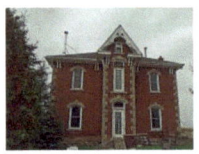